A GUIDE TO THE
BODHISATTVA WAY OF LIFE
(Bodhicaryāvatāra)

by

Śāntideva

Translated from the Sanskrit and Tibetan
by

Vesna A. Wallace
and
B. Alan Wallace

Snow Lion Publications
Ithaca, New York USA

Snow Lion Publications
P.O. Box 6483
Ithaca, New York 14851 USA
Tel: 607-273-8519

ISBN 1-55939-061-1

Library of Congress Cataloging-in-Publication Data

Śāntideva, 7th cent.
    [Bodhicaryāvatāra. English]
    A guide to the Bodhisattva way of life : Bodhicaryāvatāra / by Śāntideva ;
translated from the Sanskrit and Tibetan by Vesna A. Wallace and B. Alan
Wallace. -- 1st ed.
      p.   cm.
    Includes bibliographical references.
    ISBN 1-55939-061-1
    1. Mahayana Buddhism--Doctrines--Early works to 1800.   I. Wallace,
Vesna A. II. Wallace, B. Alan.   III. Title.
BQ3142.E5W36 1997
294.3'85--dc21   96-47279
                                               CIP

Table of Contents

Dedicated to the memory of
Venerable Geshe Ngawang Dhargyey

Preface

Śāntideva's classic treatise, the *Bodhicaryāvatāra*, translated here as *A Guide to the Bodhisattva Way of Life*, has been the most widely read, cited, and practiced text in the whole of the Indo-Tibetan Buddhist tradition. Bu ston rin chen grub, a renowned Tibetan scholar of the thirteenth century, wrote in his *History of Buddhism in India and Tibet*[1] that according to the Buddhist tradition, one hundred commentaries on the *Bodhicaryāvatāra* were extant in India, but only eight of them were translated into Tibetan. Moreover, His Holiness the Dalai Lama comments that the *Bodhicaryāvatāra* is the primary source of most of the Tibetan Buddhist literature on the cultivation of altruism and the Spirit of Awakening,[2] and his recent comprehensive work entitled *The World of Tibetan Buddhism* frequently cites this text. The *Bodhicaryāvatāra* has also been a widely known and respected text in the Buddhist tradition of Mongolia, and it was the first Buddhist text translated into classical Mongolian from Tibetan by Coiji Odser in 1305.

Although the *Bodhicaryāvatāra* has already been translated several times into English, earlier translations have been based exclusively on either Sanskrit versions or Tibetan translations. To the best of our knowledge, no earlier translation into English, including the recent

1. Bu ston, *The History of Buddhism in India and Tibet*, trans. by E. Obermiller (Delhi: Sri Satguru Publications, 1986), p. 166.

2. The Dalai Lama, *The World of Tibetan Buddhism*, trans., ed., and annot. by Geshe Thupten Jinpa (Boston: Wisdom Publications, 1995), p. 59.

translation by Kate Crosby and Andrew Skilton, has drawn from both the Sanskrit version and its authoritative Sanskrit commentary of Prajñākaramati as well as Tibetan translations and commentaries. Our present translation is based on two Sanskrit editions, namely, Louis de la Vallée Poussin's edition (1901) of the *Bodhicaryāvatāra* and the *Pañjikā* commentary of Prajñākaramati, and P. L. Vaidya's edition (1960) of the *Bodhicaryāvatāra* and the *Pañjikā* commentary; and it is also based on the Tibetan Derge edition, entitled the *Bodhisattvā-caryāvatāra*, translated by Sarvajñādeva and dPal brtsegs. We have also consulted two Tibetan commentaries to this work: *sPyod 'jug rnam bshad rgyal sras 'jug ngogs* by rGyal tshab dar ma rin chen and *Byang chub sems pa'i spyod pa la 'jug pa'i 'grel bshad rgyal sras rgya mtsho'i yon tan rin po che mi zad 'jo ba'i bum bzang* by Thub bstan chos kyi grags pa. As becomes apparent throughout the text, contrary to popular assumption, the recension incorporated into the Tibetan canon is significantly different from the Sanskrit version edited by Louis de la Vallée Poussin and P. L. Vaidya. This would seem to refute the contention of Crosby and Skilton that the canonical Tibetan translation by Blo ldan shes rab was based on the Sanskrit version available to us today. Moreover, pronouncements concerning which of the extant Sanskrit and Tibetan versions is truer to the original appear to be highly speculative, with very little basis in historical fact. This translation attempts to let these versions speak for themselves—as closely as the English allows—leaving our readers to make their own judgments concerning the degree of antiquity, authenticity, and overall coherence of the Sanskrit and Tibetan renditions of Śāntideva's classic treatise.

In terms of our methodology, we have primarily based our translation on the Sanskrit version and its commentary, though we have always consulted the Tibetan translation and its commentaries. Thus, the main text constitutes a translation of both the Sanskrit and Tibetan versions where they do not differ in content. However, in those verses where the Tibetan differs significantly from the Sanskrit, we have included English translations of the Tibetan version in footnotes to the text. Explanatory notes drawn from the *Pañjikā* commentary and other sources have also been given in footnotes to the text. Many of the Sanskrit verses of this text are concise and at times cryptic, and they often entail complex syntax. Thus, at times we were forced to take certain freedoms in our translation in order to make the English intelligible.

We hope that this translation will contribute to the greater understanding and appreciation of this classic treatise by Śāntideva, and that it will inspire others in the further study of this text and other works attributed to this great Indian Buddhist contemplative, scholar, and poet.

Vesna A. Wallace
B. Alan Wallace
Half Moon Bay, California
July 1996

Introduction

A Brief Biography of Śāntideva

Śāntideva, an eighth-century Indian Buddhist monk, is among the most renowned and esteemed figures in the entire history of Mahāyāna Buddhism. As in the case of many other figures in the history of Indian Buddhism, there is little historical knowledge of the life of Śāntideva. Two brief accounts of his life are found in Tibetan sources. One early, concise biography was composed by the great Tibetan scholar Bu ston (twelfth-thirteenth century) in his work *The History of Buddhism in India and Tibet*.[3] A later account was composed by Tāranātha (sixteenth-seventeenth century), a prominent Tibetan Buddhist scholar and historian. According to Tāranātha, Śāntideva, like Buddha Śākyamuni, was born into a royal family and was destined for the throne.[4] But on the verge of his coronation, Mañjuśrī, a divine embodiment of wisdom, and Tārā, a divine embodiment of compassion, both appeared to him in dreams and counseled him not to ascend to the throne. Thus, he left his father's kingdom, retreated to the wilderness, and devoted himself to meditation. During this

---

3. *The History of Buddhism in India and Tibet*, trans. E. Obermiller (Delhi: Sri Satguru Publications, 1986).

4. *Tāranātha's History of Buddhism in India*, trans. Lama Chimpa & Alaka Chattopadhyaya; ed. Debiprasad Chattopadhyaya (Delhi: Motilal Banarsidass, 1990), pp. 215-220.

time, he achieved advanced states of *samādhi* and various *siddhis*, and from that time forward he constantly beheld visions of Mañjuśrī, who guided him as his spiritual mentor.

After this sojourn in the wilderness, he served for awhile as minister to a king, whom he helped to rule in accordance with the principles of Buddhism. But this aroused jealousy on the part of the other ministers, and Śāntideva withdrew from the service of the king. Making his way to the renowned monastic university of Nālanda, he took monastic ordination and devoted himself to the thorough study of the Buddhist *sūtras* and *tantras*. It was during this period that he composed two other classic works: the *Śikṣasamuccaya* and the *Sūtrasamuccaya*. But as far as his fellow monks could see, all he did was eat, sleep, and defecate.

Seeking to humiliate him and thus expel him from the monastery, the other scholars compelled him to recite a *sūtra* before the monastic community and the public, a task they thought far exceeded his abilities. After some hesitation, Śāntideva agreed to the request and asked them, "Shall I recite an existing text or an original composition?" "Recite something new!" they told him, and in response he began chanting the *Bodhicaryāvatāra*. During this astonishing recital, when he came to the verse "When neither an entity nor a nonentity remains before the mind...,"[5] it is said that he rose up into the sky. Even after his body disappeared from sight, his voice completed the recitation of this text.

Different versions of this work were recorded by his listeners, and they could not come to a consensus as to which was the most accurate. Eventually, the scholars of Nālanda learned that Śāntideva had come to dwell in the city of Kaliṅga in Triliṅga, and they journeyed there to entreat him to return to the university. Although he declined, he did tell them where to find copies of his other two works, and he told them which of the versions of the *Bodhicaryāvatāra* was true to his words.

Thereafter, Śāntideva retreated to a monastery in a forest filled with wildlife. Some of the other monks noticed that at times animals would enter his cell and not come out, and they accused him of killing them. After he had demonstrated to them that no harm had come to these creatures, he once again departed, despite the pleas of his fellow

---

5. *Bodhicaryāvatāra*, IX, v. 34.

monks to remain. On this and many other occasions, Śāntideva is said to have displayed his amazing *siddhis*. From this point on, he renounced the signs of monkhood and wandered about India, devoting himself to the service of others.

Contextualization of the Bodhicaryāvatāra

At the outset of this treatise, Śāntideva denies any originality to his work, and indeed its contents conform closely to the teachings of many of the Mahāyāna *sūtras*. However, the poignancy and poetic beauty of his work belie his disavowal of any ability in composition. Due to the terse nature of his Sanskrit verses, the aesthetic quality of his treatise has been very difficult to convey in English. Therefore, in our translation, where necessary we have opted for accuracy of content over poetic quality. We hope this does not obscure the fact that the *Bodhicaryāvatāra* stands as one of the great literary and religious classics of the entire Buddhist tradition.

The thematic structure of this work is based on the six perfections of generosity, ethical discipline, patience, zeal, meditation, and wisdom, which provide the framework for the Bodhisattva's path to enlightenment. The first three chapters discuss the benefits of *bodhicitta*, the Spirit of Awakening that motivates the Bodhisattva way of life, and explain the means of cultivating and sustaining this altruistic aspiration. Those topics lay the foundation of the perfection of generosity.

The fourth and fifth chapters discuss the means of implementing the Spirit of Awakening in daily life and thereby address the perfection of ethical discipline. Chapters six, seven, and eight set forth the perfections of patience, zeal, and meditation, respectively. The sixth chapter is widely considered as a classic in its own right, for it presents a broad array of contemplations designed to counteract hatred, which is seen in the Mahāyāna as the most virulent of all the mental afflictions and the one most antithetical to the Bodhisattva way of life.

The eighth chapter, concerned with the perfection of meditation, has for its main theme the cultivation of altruism and the Spirit of Awakening. In recent years, however, this chapter has raised a certain degree of controversy on the grounds that it is misogynous. To determine whether or not that claim is justified, one must contextualize Śāntideva's discussion of a particular type of meditation that acts as an antidote to lust. Within the monastic context, the Buddhist teachings as a whole frequently address the impurity of a woman's body as a means of counteracting men's lust for women. Specifically, Śāntideva was himself a Buddhist monk, and this treatise was initially presented before an audience comprised chiefly of other Buddhist monks, who had taken vows of celibacy. From a Buddhist perspective, lust directed toward another person of either gender is not a sign of respect, regardless of the charming rhetoric that is often inspired by this mental affliction. Rather, attachment for another person actually *dehumanizes* its object by regarding this individual simply as an object for one's own gratification, rather than as a conscious subject with his or her own needs and desires.

In this eighth chapter, Śāntideva also discusses the disadvantages of attachment to *one's own impure body*. In addition, he writes of the problems of attachment to one's friends, possessions, reputation, as well as to women and *their* bodies. The central point of this entire discussion, as he points out in verse 85 of this chapter, is to become disillusioned with sensual desire. Immediately following this exposition, he addresses the main theme of this chapter, namely the meditative cultivation of altruism and the Spirit of Awakening, which embraces all beings, male and female, with love and compassion. The implication here is that insofar as one is free of self-centered craving for such things as sensual gratification, honor, and wealth, one is primed for the successful cultivation of genuine altruism.

The ninth chapter on the perfection of wisdom is one of the primary expositions in the Indian Buddhist tradition of the Prāsaṅgika Madhyamaka view, which accords with the writings of Buddhapālita and Candrakīrti. The characteristic theme of this school is that all phenomena are devoid of any intrinsic nature, for they exist purely by the power of conceptual imputation. Thus, the whole of reality is comprised of two truths: conventional truth, which consists solely of dependently related events, and ultimate truth, which is the mere absence of an intrinsic nature of those events. Following a discussion of those two truths, Śāntideva presents concise Prāsaṅgika critiques of specific views of other Buddhist schools, such as the Yogācāra and Vaibhāṣika, and non-Buddhist schools, such as the Sāṃkhya and Nyāya. He also explains the Prāsaṅgika interpretation of personal and phenomenal identitylessness and the four applications of mindfulness; and he concludes with a variety of arguments in refutation of true, or intrinsic, existence.

In the tenth, concluding chapter, Śāntideva offers prayers dedicating the merits of this work for the benefit of all sentient beings. Here he returns to his initial theme of generosity and the Spirit of Awakening, which pervades this entire treatise.

Chapter I
The Benefit of the Spirit of Awakening

Oṃ Homage to the Buddha[1]

1. Reverently bowing to the Sugatas,[2] who are endowed with the Dharmakāya, together with their Children and all who are worthy of veneration, I shall concisely present a guide to the discipline of the Children of the Sugatas in accordance with the scriptures.

---

1. The Tibetan translators substitute this homage with "Homage to all the Buddhas and Bodhisattvas" *(sangs rgyas dang byang chub sems dpa' thams cad la phyag 'tshal lo)*, signifying that this text is associated with the Buddhist *sūtras*, as opposed to the *vinaya* or *abhidharma*.

2. The *Pañjikā*, p. 1, defines the Sugatas in four ways: (1) as those who have reached the elimination of the obscurations of mental afflictions and so forth *(kleśyādyāvaraṇa-prahāṇaṃ gatāḥ)*; (2) as those who have reached the celebrated truth of the identitylessness of all phenomena *(praśastaṃ sarva-dharma-niḥsvabhāvatā-tattvaṃ gatā adhigatāḥ)*; (3) as those who have gone, not to return again *(apunar āvṛttyā gatāḥ)*, because they have completely eradicated spiritual ignorance *(avidyā)* which is the seed of grasping onto the "I" *(ahaṃkāra)*, and by that elimination of spiritual ignorance the Sugatas differ from the Stream-enterers *(srotāpanna)*, Once-returners *(sakṛd-āgamin)*, and Bodhisattvas; (4) and as those who have reached the complete elimination of every karmic imprint *(vāsanā)* without any remainder, and due to this state of complete departure, the Sugatas differ from the Non-returners *(anāgamin)*, Śrāvakas, and Pratyekabuddhas.

2.   There is nothing here that has not been said before, nor do I have any skill in composition. Thus, I have no concern for the welfare of others,[3] and I have composed this solely to season my own mind.

3.   Owing to this, the power of my faith increases to cultivate virtue. Moreover, if someone else with a disposition like my own examines this, it may be meaningful.

4.   This leisure and endowment,[4] which are so difficult to obtain, have been acquired, and they bring about the welfare of the world. If one fails to take this favorable opportunity into consideration, how could this occasion occur again?

5.   Just as lightning illuminates the darkness of a cloudy night for an instant, in the same way, by the power of the Buddha, occasionally people's minds are momentarily inclined toward merit.

6.   Thus, virtue is perpetually ever so feeble, while the power of vice is great and extremely dreadful. If there were no Spirit of Perfect Awakening, what other virtue would overcome it?

7.   The Lords of Sages, who have been contemplating for many eons, have seen this alone as a blessing by which joy is easily increased and immeasurable multitudes of beings are rescued.

---

3. The *Pañjikā*, p. 4, explains this in the following way: "Due to the insufficiency of my abilities, I do not think, 'This is conducive to the benefit of others.'"

4. "Leisure" refers here to the freedom to practice Dharma. Śāntideva is specifically referring to the eight freedoms from unfavorable "moments," which are listed in Nāgārjuna's *Suhṛllekha* vv. 63-64 (1975, p. 56). In his *Śikṣāsamuccaya* ch. 1 [2], Śāntideva mentions the eight unfavorable moments in his citation of the *Jayoṣmāyātanavimokṣa* passage in the *Gaṇḍavyūhasūtra*. These eight are described in detail in the *Mahāvyutpatti* and the *Dhammasaṅgani*.

"Endowment" refers to the conjunction of circumstances deemed essential for the successful practice of Dharma.

The *Pañjikā*, p. 5, mentions the absence of the eight non-leisures, which is difficult to obtain. It specifies them in the order in which they are listed in Śāntideva's quotation of the *Gaṇḍavyūha* in his *Śikṣāsamuccaya* (1961, p. 4): "Human existence is difficult to obtain. The purity of leisure and endowment is difficult to obtain. An encounter with a Buddha is difficult to obtain. Unimpaired sense faculties are difficult to obtain. Hearing the Buddha Dharma is difficult to obtain. Encountering good people is difficult to obtain. True spiritual friends are difficult to obtain, and attraction to the instruction regarding true conduct is difficult to obtain. A right livelihood in the world of men is difficult to obtain."

8.   Those who long to overcome the abundant miseries of mundane existence, those who wish to dispel the adversities of sentient beings, and those who yearn to experience a myriad of joys should never forsake the Spirit of Awakening.

9.   When the Spirit of Awakening has arisen, in an instant a wretch who is bound in the prison of the cycle of existence is called a Child of the Sugatas and becomes worthy of reverence in the worlds of gods and humans.

10. Upon taking this impure form, it transmutes it into the priceless image of the gem of the Jina. So, firmly hold to the quicksilver elixir, called the Spirit of Awakening, which must be utterly transmuted.

11. The world's sole leaders, whose minds are fathomless, have well examined its great value. You who are inclined to escape from the states of mundane existence, hold fast to the jewel of the Spirit of Awakening.

12. Just as a plantain tree decays upon losing its fruit, so does every other virtue wane.[5] But the tree of the Spirit of Awakening perpetually bears fruit, does not decay, and only flourishes.

13. Owing to its protection, as due to the protection of a powerful man, even after committing horrendous vices, one immediately overcomes great fears. Why do ignorant beings[6] not seek refuge in it?

14. Like the conflagration at the time of the destruction of the universe, it consumes great vices in an instant. The wise Lord Maitreya taught its incalculable benefits to Sudhana.

---

5. The *Pañjikā*, p. 9: "Just as a plantain tree, after bearing fruit for a week, does not yield fruit again, so every virtue other than the Spirit of Awakening, after some ripening, is unable to bear fruit....[The Spirit of Awakening] bears fruit all the time and does not decay, because it brings forth the attainment of joy in the state of gods and humans. Because of its steady nature, it is like a special virtue."

6. The Tibetan *bag can* can easily be mistaken for *bag yod*, meaning "conscientious." However, the corresponding Sanskrit term is *ajña*, "ignorant," which is glossed as *prajñāvikala* (deficient in wisdom) and as *mūḍha* (deluded) in the *Pañjikā* commentary, p. 10. The *Bod rgya tshig mdzod chen mo* cites the first meaning of *bag* as *bag dog po* (*sems gu dog po, sems rgya khyon cher med pa*), giving *bag can* the meaning of "small-minded." Thus, the Tibetan term does coincide with the Sanskrit.

15.   In brief, this Spirit of Awakening is known to be of two kinds: the spirit of aspiring for Awakening,[7] and the spirit of venturing toward Awakening.[8]

16.   Just as one perceives the difference between a person who yearns to travel and a traveler, so do the learned recognize the corresponding difference between those two.[9]

17.   Although the result of the spirit of aspiring for Awakening is great[10] within the cycle of existence, it is still not like the continual state of merit[11] of the spirit of venturing.

18.   From the time that one adopts that Spirit with an irreversible attitude for the sake of liberating limitless sentient beings,

19.   From that moment on, an uninterrupted stream of merit, equal to the sky, constantly arises even when one is asleep or distracted.[12]

20.   The Tathāgata himself cogently asserted this in the *Subāhupṛcchā* for the sake of beings who are inclined toward the Lesser Vehicle.

---

7. The *Pañjikā*, p. 11, defines the spirit of aspiring for Awakening (*praṇidhi-citta*) as the mind that has arisen due to aspiration but does not engage in generosity (*dāna*) and so forth. For example, there is first a thought in the form of a prayer: "May I become a Buddha in order to protect the entire world."

8. According to the *Pañjikā*, p. 11, the spirit of venturing toward Awakening (*prasthāna-citta*) is the mind that engages in actions that result in the accumulations (*saṃbhāra*) of merit (*puṇya*) and knowledge (*jñāna*).

9. The spirit of aspiring for Awakening and the spirit of venturing toward Awakening.

10. According to the *Pañjikā*, pp. 12-13, "The result that has the nature of the states of being a god and a human and that is characterized by the attainment of joy is great, that is, it is greater than any other virtue. Even when the Spirit of Awakening is devoid of good conduct, it should not be despised, for it alone brings forth happiness in the endless cycle of existence."

11. *Puṇya*, or Tib. *bsod nams*, is widely regarded in Buddhism as something that is accumulated in one's mind-stream as a result of virtuous activity, and that is diminished by non-virtuous deeds such as acts of malice. It is the source of well-being within *saṃsāra*, and its accumulation is a necessary element in the pursuit of *nirvāṇa*. Thus, it has the meaning of "spiritual power," in addition to "merit" and "virtue."

12. The Sanskrit *pramatta* is glossed in the *Pañjikā*, p. 13, as *vikṣiptacitta* (distracted), while the Tibetan translation *bag med* means "unconscientious," or "negligent."

21. A well-intentioned person who thinks, "I shall eliminate the headaches of sentient beings," bears immeasurable merit.

22. What then of a person who desires to remove the incomparable[13] pain of every single being and endow them with immeasurable good qualities?

23. Who has even a mother or father with such altruism? Would the gods, sages, or Brahmas have it?[14]

24. If those beings have never before had that wish for their own sake even in their dreams, how could they possibly have it for the sake of others?

25. How does this unprecedented and distinguished jewel,[15] whose desire for the benefit of others does not arise in others even for their own self-interest, come into existence?

26. How can one measure the merit of the jewel of the mind, which is the seed of the world's joy and is the remedy for the world's suffering?

27. If reverence for the Buddhas is exceeded merely by an altruistic intention, how much more so by striving for the complete happiness of all sentient beings?

28. Those desiring to escape from suffering hasten right toward suffering. With the very desire for happiness, out of delusion they destroy their own happiness as if it were an enemy.

29. He satisfies with all joys those who are starving for happiness and eliminates all the sorrows of those who are afflicted in many ways.

30. He dispels delusion. Where else is there such a saint? Where else is there such a friend? Where else is there such merit?

---

13. **Tibetan:** "incalculable" *(dpag tu med pa)*.

14. According to the *Pañjikā*, p. 14, "gods" refers to the Vedic gods Soma, Varuṇa, and others; "sages" refers to Hindu sages Vasiṣṭha, Gotama, and others; and "Brahmas" refers to the Hindu concept of creators.

15. According to the *Pañjikā*, p. 15, "unprecedented and distinguished jewel" refers to a sentient being.
   Tibetan: "jewel of the mind."

31.   Even one who repays a kind deed is praised somewhat, so what should be said of a Bodhisattva whose good deed is unsolicited?

32.   The world honors as virtuous one who makes a gift to a few people, even if it is merely a momentary and contemptuous donation of plain food and support for half a day.

33.   What then of one who forever bestows to countless sentient beings the fulfillment of all yearnings, which is inexhaustible until the end of beings as limitless as space?[16]

34.   The Lord declared, "One who brings forth an impure thought in his heart against a benefactor, a Child of the Jina, will dwell in hells for as many eons as there were impure thoughts."[17]

35.   But if one's mind is kindly inclined, one will bring forth an even greater fruit. Even when a greatly violent crime is committed against the Children of the Jinas, their virtue spontaneously arises.[18]

36.   I pay homage to the bodies of those in whom this precious jewel of the mind has arisen. I go for refuge to those who are mines of joy, toward whom even an offense results in happiness.

---

16. **Tibetan:** "What need be said of one who forever bestows the peerless bliss of the Sugatas and fulfills all the yearnings of countless sentient beings for all time?"

17. According to the Pañjikā, p. 18, a source of this quote is the *Gunaratnasamuccaya*.

18. **Tibetan:** "Even when great force is brought against the Children of the Jinas, it does not give rise to vice on their part, but their virtue spontaneously increases."

Chapter II
The Confession of Sin

1. In order to adopt that jewel of the mind, I make offerings to the Tathāgatas, to the stainless jewel of the sublime Dharma,[19] and to the Children of the Buddhas, who are oceans of excellent qualities.

2. As many flowers, fruits, and medicinal herbs as there are, and as many jewels as there are in the world, and clear and pleasant waters,

3. Jeweled mountains, forested regions, and other delightful and solitary places, vines shining with the ornaments of lovely flowers,[20] and trees with branches bowed with delicious fruit,

4. Fragrances and incenses, wish-fulfilling trees, jeweled trees, lakes adorned with lotuses, enchanting calls of wild geese in the worlds of gods and other celestials,

5. Uncultivated crops, planted crops, and other things that ornament the venerable ones, all these that are unowned and that extend throughout space,

---

19. The *Pañjikā*, p. 12: "The jewel of sublime Dharma that is characterized by scriptures and spiritual realizations *(āgamādhigama-lakṣaṇa)*."

20. **Tibetan:** "shrubs adorned with flowers."

6.   I bring to mind and offer to the Foremost of Sages together with their Children. May those worthy of precious gifts, the greatly merciful ones, compassionate toward me, accept these from me.

7.   Devoid of merit and destitute, I have nothing else to offer. Therefore, may the Protectors, whose concerns are for the welfare of others, accept this by their own power for my sake.

8.   I completely offer my entire self[21] to the Jinas and their Children. O Supreme Beings, accept me! I reverently devote myself to your service.

9.   Being free from fear of mundane existence due to your protection, I shall serve sentient beings; I shall completely transcend my earlier vices, and henceforth I shall sin[22] no more.

10.   In sweetly fragrant bathing chambers whose beautiful pillars are radiant with jewels, glowing canopies made of pearls, and crystal floors transparent and sparkling,

11.   I bathe the Tathāgatas and their Children with many vases studded with superb jewels and filled with pleasing, fragrant flowers and water, to the accompaniment of songs and instrumental music.[23]

---

21. **Tibetan:** "I offer my body...."

22. Throughout this text, Śāntideva addresses the issue of sin (*pāpa, sdig pa*) on many occasions. Modern Western readers commonly reject the introduction of the word *sin* into Buddhist translations on the grounds that it is too heavily laden with theological and psychological nuances from the history of Western religions and society. The word is so closely associated, they argue, with divine retribution, guilt, and fear that it should be avoided altogether in Buddhist writings.

In this work we have translated the term *pāpa* both as *sin* and as *vice*. Although there are other possible translations—including *misdeed, fault, offense, transgression,* or *wrongdoing*—none of these corresponds as closely to this Buddhist concept. In both the *Bodhicaryāvatāra* and the *Sikṣāsamuccaya* Śāntideva distinguishes between the terms *pāpa, āpatti,* and *doṣa*. Whereas *pāpa* refers to every non-virtuous deed (*akuśala-karma*), *āpatti* refers only to downfalls in terms of the transgression of precepts; and *doṣa* refers to a wide array of faults, including detrimental character traits, and not just non-virtuous acts. Thus, the terms *offense, transgression,* and *fault* do not have the same meaning as *pāpa*. The English terms *misdeed* and *wrongdoing* do correspond reasonably well to the meaning of *pāpa*, but considering Śāntideva's emphasis on confessing and purifying *pāpa* to avoid its dire consequences, such as rebirth in hell, the English usage of *sin* seems to correspond most closely to this Sanskrit term.

23. **Tibetan:** "...I bathe the Tathāgatas and their Children with many vases filled with pleasing, aromatic water."

12.   I dry their bodies with scented, immaculate, exquisite cloths; then I offer them beautifully colored and sweetly fragrant garments.

13.   I adorn Samantabhadra, Ajita, Mañjughoṣa, Lokeśvara,[24] and others with those divine, soft, delicate, and colorful raiments and with the most precious of jewels.[25]

14.   With perfumes permeating a thousand million worlds, I anoint the bodies of the Lords of Sages that are blazing with the luster of well-refined, rubbed, and polished gold.

15.   I worship the most glorious Lords of Sages with all wonderfully fragrant and pleasing blossoms—*māndārava* flowers,[26] blue lotuses, and others—and with splendidly arranged garlands.

16.   I perfume them with enchanting clouds of incenses having a pungent and pervasive aroma. I offer them feasts consisting of various foods and drinks.

17.   I offer them jeweled lamps, mounted in rows on golden lotuses; and I scatter lovely drifts of blossoms on the floor anointed with perfume.

18.   To those filled with love I also offer brilliant multitudes of palaces, delightful with songs of praise, radiant with garlands of pearls and jewels, and ornamented at the entrances in four directions.

19.   I bring to mind the great sages' exquisitely beautiful, jeweled parasols perfectly raised with golden handles, lovely shapes, and inlaid pearls.

20.   Thereafter, may delightful clouds of offerings rise high, and clouds of instrumental music that enrapture all sentient beings.

---

24. Ajita is another name for Maitreya. It is omitted in the Tibetan translation. Lokeśvara is another name for Avalokiteśvara.

25. **Tibetan:** "...with hundreds of supreme jewels."

26. According to the *Pañjikā*, p. 26, *māndārava* is a kind of flower that is found in the realm of gods.

21.   May showers of flowers, jewels, and the like continually fall on the images, reliquaries, and all the jewels of the sublime Dharma.[27]

22.   Just as Mañjughoṣa and others[28] worship the Jinas, so do I worship the Tathāgatas, the Protectors, together with their Children.

23.   With hymns that are seas of melodies, I praise the Oceans of Virtues. May the clouds of harmonies of praise ascend to them in the same way.

24.   With prostrations as numerous as the atoms within all the Buddha-fields, I bow to the Buddhas present in all the three times, to the Dharma, and to the Sublime Assembly.

25.   Likewise, I pay homage to all the shrines and to the resting-places[29] of the Bodhisattva. I prostrate to the preceptors and to the praiseworthy adepts as well.[30]

26.   I go for refuge to the Buddha as far as the quintessence of enlightenment; I go for refuge to the Dharma and the community of Bodhisattvas.[31]

27.   With folded hands I beseech the Fully Awakened Ones present in all directions and the greatly compassionate Bodhisattvas.

---

27. According to the *Pañjikā*, p. 27, the phrase "and so on" implies "the showers of sandal paste, aromatic powder, cloths, etc."; and "the jewels of the sublime Dharma" refers to the twelve scriptural categories *(dvādaśāṅga-pravacana)*. For the list of the twelve divisions, see Hirakawa Akira, *A History of Indian Buddhism from Śākyamuni to Early Mahāyāna* (University of Hawaii, 1990), p. 75.

28. The *Pañjikā*, p. 28: "The foremost among the Protectors of the world, Mañjughoṣa, Samantabhadra, and Ajita, the Bodhisattvas who are the masters of ten Grounds *(daśa-bhūmi)*."

29. The *Pañjikā*, p. 28, states that "the shrines" *(caitya)* refers to the *stūpas* with and without relics, and "the resting-places" *(āśraya)* refers to the places of the Buddha's birth and so on, as narrated in the *Jātaka* and *Avadāna* accounts. The commentary also indicates that this particular rule of worship is described in the *Trisamayarājasūtra* and the *Āryaratnameghasūtra*.

30. **Tibetan:** "I prostrate to the preceptors, as well as teachers and adepts."

31. The *Pañjikā*, p. 29, explains that going for refuge means "keeping the injunctions of that [refuge], that is, one does not transgress the injunctions of the one in whom one takes refuge."

28.   Whatever sin I, a brute, have committed or caused others to commit in this life and others throughout the beginningless cycle of existence,

29.   And anything in which I have deludedly rejoiced, thereby harming myself—that transgression I confess, overcome by remorse.[32]

30.   Whatever offense I have committed, out of disrespect, with my body, speech, and mind against the Three Jewels, against mothers and fathers, and against spiritual mentors and others,

31.   And whatever terrible vices I, a sinner, defiled with many faults, have done, O Guides, I confess them all.

32.   How shall I escape it? Rescue me quickly! May death not soon creep up on me before my vices have vanished.

33.   Death does not differentiate between tasks done and undone. This traitor is not to be trusted by the healthy or the ill, for it is like an unexpected, great thunderbolt.[33]

34.   I have committed various vices for the sake of friends and enemies. This I have not recognized: "Leaving everyone behind, I must pass away."

35.   My enemies will not remain, nor will my friends remain. I shall not remain. Nothing will remain.

36.   Whatever is experienced will fade to a memory. Like an experience in a dream, everything that has passed will not be seen again.[34]

---

32. **Tibetan:** "Whatever sin I have committed unknowingly or caused others to commit in this or other lives in the beginningless cycle of existence, and in which I have rejoiced due to being oppressed by the deception of delusion—that transgression I have seen, and I earnestly confess it to the Lords."

33. **Tibetan:** "This capricious Lord of Death does not wait for things done and left undone. No one, neither the ill nor the healthy, can depend on this transient life."

34. **Tibetan:** "Like experience in dreams, whatever is experienced is reduced to a memory, and all that is past is seen no more."

37.   Even in this life, as I have stood by, many friends and enemies have passed away, but terrible sin induced by them remains ahead of me.

38.   Thus, I have not considered that I am ephemeral. Due to delusion, attachment, and hatred, I have sinned in many ways.

39.   Day and night, a life span unceasingly diminishes, and there is no adding onto it. Shall I not die then?[35]

40.   Although lying here on a bed and relying on relatives, I alone have to bear the feeling of being cut off from my vitality.

41.   For a person seized by the messengers of Death, what good is a relative and what good is a friend? At that time, merit alone is a protection, and I have not applied myself to it.

42.   O Protectors, I, negligent and unaware of this danger, have acquired many vices out of attachment to this transient life.[36]

43.   One completely languishes while being led today to have the limbs of one's body amputated. Parched with thirst, and with pitiable eyes, one sees the world differently.

44.   How much more is one overpowered by the horrifying appearances of the messengers of Death as one is consumed by the fever of terror and smeared with a mass of excrement?[37]

45.   With distressed glances I seek protection in the four directions. Which good person will be my protection from this great fear?

46.   Seeing the four directions devoid of protection, I return to confusion.[38] What shall I do in that state of great fear?

---

35. **Tibetan:** "How shall one like me not die?"

36. **Tibetan:** "...for the sake of this transient life."

37. **Tibetan:** "What need, then, is there to speak of the pathos of one who is overpowered by the terrifying forms of the messengers of the Lord of Death, and who is stricken with the affliction of great dread?"

38. **Tibetan:** "despair" (*kun tu yi mug*).

47.   Right now I go for refuge to the Protectors of the World whose power is great, to the Jinas, who strive to protect the world and who eliminate every fear.

48.   Likewise, I earnestly go for refuge to the Dharma that is mastered by them and that annihilates the fear of the cycle of existence, and to the assembly of Bodhisattvas as well.

49.   Trembling with fear, I offer myself to Samantabhadra, and of my own will I offer myself to Mañjughoṣa.[39]

50.   Terrified, I utter a mournful cry to the Protector Avalokita, whose conduct overflows with compassion, that he may protect me, a sinner.[40]

51.   Seeking protection, I earnestly invoke noble Ākāśagarbha, Kṣitigarbha, and all the Compassionate Ones.

52.   I bow to Vajrī, upon the sight of whom the messengers of Death and other malevolent beings[41] flee in terror to the four directions.[42]

53.   After neglecting your counsel, in terror I go to you for refuge now as I face this fear. Swiftly remove my fear!

54.   Even one frightened by a fleeting illness would not disregard the physician's advice; how much more so one afflicted by the four hundred and four diseases,[43]

---

39. **Tibetan:** "Distraught with fear, I offer myself to Samantabhadra, and I offer my body to Mañjughoṣa."

40. **Tibetan:** "And to Lord Avalokiteśvara, whose compassionate conduct is unfailing, I make the mournful plea, 'Protect me, the sinner!'"

41. According to the *Pañjikā*, p. 33, "Vajrī" here refers to Vajrapāṇi, and "others" refers to Yakṣas, Rākṣasas, etc.

42. **Tibetan:** "I take refuge in Vajrī, upon the sight of whom the evil messengers of the Lord of Death flee in terror to the four directions."

43. **Tibetan:** "When frightened by an ordinary illness, if it is necessary to heed the physician's advice, what need to speak of one who is continually afflicted by the hundred ailments of attachment and so on?"

55.   Of which just one can annihilate all people living in Jambudvīpa, and for which a medicine is not found in any region.[44]

56.   If I disregard the counsel of the Omniscient Physician who removes every pain, shame on me, extremely deluded one that I am![45]

57.   If I stand very attentive even on a smaller cliff, then how much more so on an enduring chasm of a thousand leagues?[46]

58.   It is inappropriate for me to be at ease, thinking, "Just today death will not arrive." The time when I will not exist is inevitable.

59.   Who can give me fearlessness? How shall I escape? I shall certainly not exist. Why is my mind at ease?

60.   What of value has remained with me from earlier experiences, which have disappeared, and engrossed in which I neglected the counsel of spiritual mentors?

---

44. According to the *Pañjikā*, p. 34, this is an allusion to a *Jātaka* story about Padmaka, a king of Rāśi. The *Pañjikā* commentary reads: "As it has been heard: A long time ago, the Bhagavān, while living the life of a Bodhisattva, was a king of Rāśi, called Padma. At that time, all the people of Jambudvīpa became afflicted with a violent disease and were dying. They thought this: 'This lord of ours, the greatly compassionate king, will provide a remedy. We shall inform him about our suffering.' Upon deciding in this way and meeting [with the king], they made their suffering known to him: 'O great king, this is our situation with relevance to you, the lord, who wishes us supreme well-being.' The king, whose heart was moved by compassion, was unable to bear their suffering and ordered the physicians: 'Swiftly eliminate their suffering caused by illness.' Having promised to do so, upon looking into treatises on medical treatments and not finding the medicine other than the fresh meat of Rohita fish, they reported so to the king, etc. This very *Jātaka* is indicated as being a description of mundane existence."

45. **Tibetan:** "If just one of them destroys all the people living in Jambudvīpa, and if no other medicine to cure them is found anywhere, then the intention not to heed the counsel of the Omniscient Physician who removes every pain is utterly deluded and shameful."

46. According to the *Pañjikā*, p. 35, "an enduring chasm of a thousand leagues" refers to the chasm of Avīci hell and so on.
     Tibetan: "If I need to stay very attentive at the edge of even a small cliff, how much more is this the case at the edge of an enduring chasm that descends for a thousand leagues?"

61.   Upon forsaking my relatives and friends and this world of the living, alone I shall go elsewhere. What is the use of all my friends and enemies?

62.   In that case, only this concern is appropriate for me day and night: How shall I surely escape suffering on account of that nonvirtue?

63.   Whatever vice, whatever natural misdeed, and whatever misdeed by prohibition[47] I, an ignorant fool, have accumulated,

64.   Terrified of suffering, all this I confess, standing with folded hands in the presence of the Protectors and bowing repeatedly.

65.   May the Guides be aware of my transgressions together with my iniquity. O Protectors, may I not commit this evil again!

---

47. Natural misdeeds (*prakṛtyāvadya*) include the ten non-virtuous actions such as killing, stealing, and so on, which are sinful for anyone who commits them. Misdeeds by prohibition (*prajñapty-avadya*) are non-virtuous only for those who have taken precepts that specifically prohibit such actions. An example would be eating at an inappropriate time, which is a misdeed for Buddhist monks but not for the laity.

Chapter III
Adopting the Spirit of Awakening

1. I happily rejoice in the virtue of all sentient beings, which relieves the suffering of the miserable states of existence. May those who suffer dwell in happiness.[48]

2. I rejoice in sentient beings' liberation from the suffering of the cycle of existence, and I rejoice in the Protectors' Bodhisattvahood and Buddhahood.

3. I rejoice in the teachers' oceanic expressions of the Spirit of Awakening, which delight and benefit all sentient beings.[49]

4. With folded hands I beseech the Fully Awakened Ones in all directions that they may kindle the light of Dharma for those who fall into suffering owing to confusion.

---

48. **Tibetan:** "I happily rejoice in the virtue done by all sentient beings, which relieves the suffering of the miserable states of existence and in the well-being of those subject to suffering." This verse is followed in the Tibetan by an additional line, not found in the Sanskrit version, and is translated here in the following way: "I rejoice in the accumulated virtue that acts as a cause for enlightenment."

49. **Tibetan:** "I happily rejoice in the oceanic virtue of cultivating the Spirit of Awakening, which delights and benefits all sentient beings."

5.   With folded hands I supplicate the Jinas who wish to leave for *nirvāṇa* that they may stay for countless eons, and that this world may not remain in darkness.

6.   May the virtue that I have acquired by doing all this[50] relieve every suffering of sentient beings.

7.   May I be the medicine and the physician for the sick. May I be their nurse until their illness never recurs.[51]

8.   With showers of food and drink may I overcome the afflictions of hunger and thirst. May I become food and drink during times of famine.

9.   May I be an inexhaustible treasury for the destitute. With various forms of assistance may I remain in their presence.

10.   For the sake of accomplishing the welfare of all sentient beings, I freely give up my body, enjoyments, and all my virtues of the three times.

11.   Surrendering everything is *nirvāṇa*, and my mind seeks *nirvāṇa*. If I must surrender everything, it is better that I give it to sentient beings.[52]

12.   For the sake of all beings I have made this body pleasureless. Let them continually beat it, revile it, and cover it with filth.[53]

13.   Let them play with my body. Let them laugh at it and ridicule it. What does it matter to me? I have given my body to them.[54]

---

50. The *Pañjikā*, p. 38: "Worship, disclosure of sin, rejoicing in virtue, etc."

51. **Tibetan:** "For as long as beings are ill and until their illnesses are cured, may I be their physician and their medicine and their nurse."

52. **Tibetan:** "As a result of surrendering everything, there is *nirvāṇa*, [and] my mind seeks *nirvāṇa*. Surrendering everything at once—this is the greatest gift to sentient beings."

53. **Tibetan:** "I have already given this body to all beings for them to do with it what they like. So at any time they may kill it, revile it, or beat it as they wish."

54. **Tibetan:** "Even if they play with my body, or use it as a source of jest or ridicule, since my body has already been given up, why should I hold it dear?"

14. Let them have me perform deeds that are conducive to their happiness.[55] Whoever resorts to me, may it never be in vain.

15. For those who have resorted to me and have an angry or unkind thought, may even that always be the cause for their accomplishing every goal.[56]

16. May those who falsely accuse me, who harm me, and who ridicule me all partake of Awakening.

17. May I be a protector for those who are without protectors, a guide for travelers, and a boat, a bridge, and a ship for those who wish to cross over.

18. May I be a lamp for those who seek light, a bed for those who seek rest, and may I be a servant for all beings who desire a servant.[57]

19. To all sentient beings may I be a wish-fulfilling gem, a vase of good fortune, an efficacious mantra, a great medication, a wish-fulfilling tree, and a wish-granting cow.

20. Just as earth and other elements are useful in various ways to innumerable sentient beings dwelling throughout infinite space,[58]

21. So may I be in various ways a source of life for the sentient beings present throughout space until they are all liberated.

22. Just as the Sugatas of old adopted the Spirit of Awakening, and just as they properly conformed to the practice of the Bodhisattvas,

---

55. **Tibetan:** "Let them do anything that does not bring them harm."

56. **Tibetan:** "Whether they look at me with anger or admiration, may this always be a cause for their accomplishing all their goals."

57. **Tibetan:** "May I be an island for those seeking an island, a lamp for those seeking light, a bed for those seeking repose, and a servant for all those beings desiring a servant."

58. **Tibetan:** "Like the great elements such as earth and space, may I always serve as the basis of the various requisites of life for innumerable sentient beings."

23. So I myself shall generate the Spirit of Awakening for the sake of the world; and so I myself shall properly engage in those practices.

24. Upon gladly adopting the Spirit of Awakening in this way, an intelligent person should thus nurture the Spirit in order to fulfill his wish.[59]

25. Now my life is fruitful. Human existence is well obtained. Today I have been born into the family of the Buddhas. Now I am a Child of the Buddha.

26. Thus, whatever I do now should accord with [the Bodhisattvas'] family, and it should not be like a stain on this pure family.[60]

27. Just as a blind man might find a jewel amongst heaps of rubbish, so this Spirit of Awakening has somehow arisen in me.

28. It is the elixir of life produced to vanquish death in the world.[61] It is an inexhaustible treasure eliminating the poverty of the world.

29. It is the supreme medicine that alleviates the illness of the world. It is the tree of rest for beings exhausted from wandering on the pathways of mundane existence.

30. It is the universal bridge for all travelers on their crossing over miserable states of existence.[62] It is the rising moon of the mind that soothes the mental afflictions of the world.

---

59. **Tibetan:** "Having joyfully adopted the Spirit of Awakening, in order to apply and increase it, an intelligent person should exalt this mind like this."

60. **Tibetan:** "Now, by every means, I shall behave in accordance with this family, and it should not be as if I have contaminated this flawless noble heritage."

61. **Tibetan:** "It is the supreme elixir of life that conquers the Lord of Death."

62. **Tibetan:** "It is the universal bridge that liberates all beings from miserable states of existence."

31. It is the great sun dispelling the darkness of the world's ignorance. It is the fresh butter formed from churning the milk of Dharma.

32. For the caravan of beings traveling on the path of mundane existence and starving for the meal of happiness, it is the feast of happiness that satisfies all sentient beings who have come as guests.[63]

33. Today I invite the world to Sugatahood and temporal happiness. May the gods, *asuras*, and others rejoice in the presence of all the Protectors!

---

63. **Tibetan:** "For the caravan of beings traveling on the path of mundane existence and longing to experience the bounties of happiness, this is the immanent supreme joy that satisfies sentient beings who have come as guests."

Chapter IV
Attending to the Spirit of Awakening[64]

1. Thus, upon firmly adopting the Spirit of Awakening, a Child of the Jinas should always vigilantly strive not to neglect his training.

2. Although one has made a commitment, it is appropriate [to reconsider] whether or not to do that which has been rashly undertaken and which has not been well considered.

3. But shall I discard that which has been examined by the sagacious Buddhas and their Children, as well as by myself according to the best of my abilities?

4. If, upon making such a promise, I do not put it into action, then having deceived those sentient beings, what destiny shall I have?

5. It has been said that a person who intended to give away even a tiny thing but does not do so becomes a *preta*.

6. Then all the more so, having deceived the entire world after loudly and sincerely inviting it to unsurpassable happiness, what state of existence shall I have?[65]

---

64. The Tibetan title to this chapter is "Teachings on Conscientiousness."

65. **Tibetan:** "Then, if I were to deceive all beings after sincerely inviting them to unsurpassable happiness, how could I ever proceed to a favorable state of existence?"

7.   Only the Omniscient One knows the inconceivable course of action of those people whom he liberates even when they forsake the Spirit of Awakening.

8.   Therefore, for a Bodhisattva it is the heaviest downfall of all; for if he commits such a downfall, he impairs the welfare of all sentient beings.

9.   If someone else hinders his virtue, even for a moment, there will be no end to his miserable states of existence, because he diminishes the welfare of sentient beings.

10.   One would be destroyed, obliterating the well-being of even one sentient being; how much more so of beings dwelling throughout all of space?

11.   Thus, due to the power of downfalls and due to the power of the Spirit of Awakening, one revolving in the cycle of existence is slow in attaining the Bodhisattva Grounds.

12.   Therefore, I should respectfully act in accordance with my commitment. If I do not make an effort now, I shall go from lower to lower states.

13.   Innumerable Buddhas have gone by, seeking out every sentient being;[66] but through my own fault, I have not come into the domain of their cure.

14.   If I remain like this, as I am now, I will repeatedly come to the miserable states of existence, illness, death, amputation, destruction, and the like.

15.   When shall I encounter the extremely rare appearance of the Tathāgata, faith, human existence, and the ability to practice virtue,

16.   Health, daily sustenance, and lack of adversity? Life is momentary and deceptive; and the body is as if on loan.[67]

---

66. **Tibetan:** "Innumerable Buddhas have gone by who have served all sentient beings...."

67. **Tibetan:** "Although on such a day as this I am free of illness, well nourished, and unafflicted, life is momentary and deceptive; and the body is as if on loan for an instant."

17. With such behavior on my part, a human state is certainly not obtained again. When a human state is not achieved, there is only vice; and how could there be blessing?[68]

18. If I do not perform virtue even when I am capable of it, what then shall I do when fully dazed by the sufferings of miserable states of existence?[69]

19. For one who does not perform virtue but accumulates sin, even the expression "favorable state of existence" will be lost for a thousand million eons.

20. Therefore, the Blessed One stated that human existence is extremely difficult to obtain, like a turtle's head emerging into the ring of a yoke on a vast ocean.

21. One dwells in the Avici hell for an eon as a consequence of a vice committed in a single moment. What then can be said of a favorable state of existence, since sin has been accumulated since beginningless time?

22. Having experienced that alone, one is still not liberated. Therefore, while experiencing it, one begets more vices.

23. Upon obtaining such leisure, if I do not practice virtue, then there is no duplicity greater than this, and there is no delusion greater than this.

24. If I recognize this and still deludedly fall into sloth, then when I am commanded by the messengers of Yama, I shall long remain in great anguish.[70]

25. The unendurable fire of hell will scorch my body for ages, and afterward the fire of remorse will torment my undisciplined mind for a long time.[71]

---

68. **Tibetan:** "…there is only vice, and no virtue."

69. **Tibetan:** "If I do not perform virtue even when I have the opportunity to do so, what shall I do when I am dazed by the sufferings of the miserable states of existence?"

70. **Tibetan:** "If I recognize this and still I deludedly fall into sloth, when death is nigh, great anguish will arise."

71. **Tibetan:** "If the unendurable fire of hell scorches my body for ages, the flames of unbearable remorse will surely torment my mind."

26.   I have somehow obtained the advantageous state that is very difficult to achieve, and though aware of that, I am led back to those same hells.

27.   I have no will in this matter, as if bewitched by spells. I do not know by whom I am bewitched or who dwells inside me.

28.   Enemies such as craving and hatred are without arms, legs, and so on. They are neither courageous nor wise. How is it that they have enslaved me?

29.   Stationed in my mind, they ruin me, while remaining well-established themselves; and yet I do not get angry at my forbearance with this shameful and improper situation.

30.   If all gods and humans[72] were my enemies, even they would be unable to bring me to the fire of the Avici hell.

31.   When encountered, it consumes even the ashes of Mount Meru. Mental afflictions, the mighty enemies, instantly throw me there.

32.   For the longevity of all other enemies is not so enduring, beginningless, and endless as that of my enemies, the mental afflictions.[73]

33.   Everyone becomes favorably disposed when tended with kindness, but when these mental afflictions are honored, they bring about suffering all the more.[74]

34.   How can I take delight in the cycle of existence when constant, long-lasting enemies, who are the sole cause of the currents and floods of adversities, fearlessly dwell in my heart?[75]

---

72. **Tibetan:** "If all gods and demigods...."

73. **Tibetan:** "All other enemies cannot remain as long as my enemies, the mental afflictions, which long endure, without beginning or end."

74. **Tibetan:** "When properly honored, everyone provides service and causes happiness, but when these mental afflictions are honored, they inflict suffering all over again."

75. **Tibetan:** "...who are the sole cause of the perpetuation of a mass of adversities...."

35. How can I be happy if the guardians of the prison of the cycle of existence, these murderers and slaughterers in hells and the like, remain in the cage of greed within the dwelling of my heart?

36. Therefore, as long as these enemies are not destroyed before my eyes, I shall not forsake my task. Those lofty with pride, who are enraged at someone who gives them even a minor insult, will not sleep until they kill him.

37. At the height of a battle, ready to slaughter those who are in darkness and who are naturally subject to suffering through death, those afflicted with injuries from countless spears and arrows do not turn back without accomplishing their goal.[76]

38. What then when I am eager to destroy my natural enemies, which are the perpetual cause of all miseries? Today, even if I am [beset] with a hundred adversities, why am I weary and despondent?[77]

39. If they wear scars from their enemies for no reason as if they were ornaments, then why do sufferings trouble me when I am set to accomplish a great goal?

40. If fishermen, outcasts, farmers, and others, whose minds are fixed merely on their own livelihoods, withstand the adversities of cold and heat, then why do I not endure for the sake of the well-being of the world?

41. While I have promised to liberate beings throughout space in the ten directions from their mental afflictions, I have not liberated even myself from mental afflictions.

---

76. **Tibetan:** "At the height of battle, utterly intent on killing those who are afflicted and who are naturally subject to suffering through death, some ignore their own injuries from arrows and spears, and do not turn back without having accomplished their goal."

77. **Tibetan:** "Then, needless to say, not even a hundred causes of suffering will make me succumb to weariness and despair as I now apply myself to conquering my natural enemies, which are the perpetual causes of all miseries."

42.   Without knowing my own limitations, I spoke at that time as if I were a bit insane. Therefore, I shall never turn back from vanquishing mental afflictions.[78]

43.   I shall be tenacious in this matter; and fixed on revenge, I shall wage war, except against those mental afflictions that are related to the elimination of mental afflictions.[79]

44.   Let my entrails ooze out and my head fall off, but by no means shall I bow down to my enemies, the mental afflictions.[80]

45.   Even if exiled, an enemy may acquire a residence and followers in another country whence he returns with his full strength. But there is no such course for the enemy, the mental afflictions.[81]

46.   Once the affliction that dwells in my mind has been expelled, where would it go, and where would it rest and attempt to destroy me? Feeble in spirit, I am lacking in perseverance. Mental afflictions are frail and conquerable with the eye of wisdom.[82]

47.   Mental afflictions do not exist in sense objects, nor in the sense faculties, nor in the space between, nor anywhere else. Then where do they exist and agitate the whole world? This is an illusion only.[83] Liberate your fearing heart and cultivate perseverance for the sake of wisdom. Why would you torture yourself in hells for no reason?[84]

---

78. **Tibetan:** "Was I not insane to speak without recognizing my own limitations...."

79. **Tibetan:** "Here I am obsessed, and with vengeance I shall wage battle. That kind of mental affliction is the exception, for it destroys mental afflictions."

80. **Tibetan:** "Let me be burned, let me perish and be beheaded, but in no way shall I submit to my enemies, the mental afflictions."

81. **Tibetan:** "Even when ordinary enemies have been expelled from one country, they settle in another and take control. Then, upon recovering their strength, they return; but the way of this enemy, the mental afflictions, is not like that."

82. **Tibetan:** "Miserable afflictions are conquerable with the eye of wisdom. Once they are dispelled from my mind, where will they go? Where would they rest and then return to torment me? Feeble in spirit, I am lacking in perseverance."

83. The *Pañjikā*, p. 47: "Hence, on account of not having a root, [mental afflictions] are empty in nature and adventitious (*āgantuka*), because they are brought forth only by false assumptions."

48.   After pondering in this way, I shall make an effort to apply the teachings as they have been explained. How can someone who could be cured by medicine be restored to health if he strays from the physician's advice?

---

84. **Tibetan:** "...This is like an illusion, so I shall abandon the fear in my heart and cultivate perseverance in the pursuit of wisdom. Why should I torture myself in hells and the like for no reason?"

Chapter V
Guarding Introspection

1. Those who wish to protect their practice should zealously guard the mind. The practice cannot be protected without guarding the unsteady mind.

2. Untamed, mad elephants do not inflict as much harm in this world as does the unleashed elephant of the mind in the Avici hell and the like.

3. But if the elephant of the mind is completely restrained by the rope of mindfulness, then all perils vanish and complete well-being is obtained.

4–5. Tigers, lions, elephants, bears, snakes, all enemies, all guardians of hells, ḍākinīs,[85] and demons become controlled by controlling the mind alone. By subduing the mind alone, they all become subdued.

6. For the Propounder of the Truth said that all fears and immeasurable sufferings arise from the mind only.

---

85. **Tibetan** reads "evil spirits" (byad ma) instead of ḍākinīs.

7.   Who diligently constructed the weapons in hell? Who devised the floor of heated iron? And from where have those women come?[86]

8.   The Sage declared that all of that has arisen from the evil mind, so there is nothing else in the three worlds more formidable than the mind.

9.   If the perfection of generosity makes the world free of poverty, how is it possible that the Protectors of the past acquired it, when the world is still impoverished today?

10. The perfection of generosity is interpreted simply as a state of mind due to the intention of giving away everything, together with the fruits of that, to all people.[87]

11. Where can fish and the like be taken where I could not kill them?[88] When the mind of renunciation is obtained, that is considered the perfection of ethical discipline.[89]

---

86. According to the *Pañjikā*, p. 52, "those women" refers to women who are seen together with their partners in adultery above and below a silk-cotton (*śālmalī*) tree. The Tibetan commentary *sPyod 'jug gi 'grel bshad rgyal sras yon tan bum bzang* explains that in a certain hell a group of women is seen climbing up and down a silk-cotton tree (Tibetan reads: "śalmari"), which is a tall tree covered with thorns. All those women are created by the past, sinful intention to engage in adultery. *Kūṭa-śālmalī* is a species of a cotton-tree (*Andersonia rohitaka*) with sharp thorns, regarded as an implement of torture in hell.

87. The *Pañjikā*, p. 53: "When, the mind that is free of the stain of envy arises on account of the absence of attachment, then the perfection of generosity emerges. Therefore, that [perfection of generosity] is simply a state of mind; and there is no other perfection of generosity."
    Tibetan: "Due to the intention of giving away everything together with the fruits [of giving] to all people, there is said to be the perfection of generosity. Thus, it is simply a state of mind."

88. The *Pañjikā*, p. 53, explains this line in the following way: "Ethical discipline (*śila*) is the mind desisting from all vices, beginning with killing, and so forth. The nature of that [ethical discipline] is not a disappearance of external objects, which are the basis [of killing and so on]. If ethical discipline arises from the absence of killing, that is, on account of the absence of beings that are the objects of killing and so on, then where can fish and the like be taken where one could not see them? Otherwise, if one starts to kill them, ethical discipline will not arise."

89. According to the *Pañjikā*, p. 53, "the mind of renunciation" refers to the mind in which all mental engagement has ceased (*nivṛtti-manasikāra*).
    Tibetan: "Where is the killing of fish and so on prevented? The perfection of ethical discipline is explained in terms of achieving a mind of renunciation."

12. How many malicious people, as [unending] as space, can I kill? When the mind-state of anger is slain, then all enemies are slain.[90]

13. Where would there be leather enough to cover the entire world? The earth is covered over merely with the leather of my sandals.[91]

14. Likewise, I am unable to restrain external phenomena, but I shall restrain my own mind. What need is there to restrain anything else?

15. Even when accompanied by body and speech, feeble mental activity does not have results such as Brahmahood and alike, which the mind alone has when it is clear.

16. The Omniscient One stated that all recitations and austerities, even though performed for a long time, are actually useless if the mind is on something else or is dull.

17. Those who have not cultivated the mind, which is the mystery and the very essence of Dharma, uselessly wander in space in order to eliminate suffering and find happiness.[92]

18. Therefore, I should well control and well guard my mind.[93] Once I have forsaken the vow of guarding the mind, of what use are many vows to me?

19. Just as those standing in the midst of boisterous people carefully guard their wounds, so those standing in the midst of evil people should always guard the wounds of their minds.

---

90. **Tibetan:** "Malicious people, as [unending] as space, cannot possibly be overcome. If this mind-state of anger is conquered, it is like vanquishing all enemies." This and the next two verses concern the perfection of patience.

91. **Tibetan:** "...With just the leather of my sandals, it is as if the whole earth were covered."

92. **Tibetan:** "Those who do not understand this mystery of the mind, which is the great principle of Dharma, wander aimlessly, even though they wish to achieve happiness and overcome suffering."

93. According to the *Pañjikā*, p. 55, one should control the mind with mindfulness (*smṛti*) and guard it with introspection (*saṃprajanya*).

20. Fearing slight pain from a wound, I guard it with great care. Why don't I, fearing the crushing of the mountains of the Saṃghāta hell, guard the wound of my mind?

21. Living with this attitude even among evil people and among maidens, with steadfast effort, a persevering sage will not be defeated.

22. Let my possessions freely vanish; let my honor, my body, livelihood, and everything else pass away. But may my virtuous mind never be lost.[94]

23. I appeal to those desiring to guard their minds: always diligently guard your mindfulness and introspection.

24. Just as a person smitten by disease is unfit for any work, so the mind lacking those two is not fit for any work.[95]

25. What has been heard, pondered, and cultivated, like water in a cracked jar, does not remain in the memory of the mind that lacks introspection.

26. Even many learned people who have faith and extraordinary perseverance become defiled by vices on account of the fault of lacking introspection.

27. Even upon accumulating virtues, those who have been robbed by the thief of non-introspection, who comes after the loss of mindfulness, enter miserable states of existence.

28. This band of thieves, the mental afflictions, looks for an entrance. Upon finding an entrance, it plunders and destroys life in fortunate realms of existence.

29. Therefore, mindfulness should never be displaced from the gate of the mind. If it is gone, it should be reinstated while recalling the anguish of hell.[96]

---

94. **Tibetan:** "Let my possessions, honor, body, and livelihood vanish; and let even other virtues decline, but may my mind never degenerate."

95. **Tibetan:** "Just as people perturbed by disease are disabled for any work, so the mind agitated by stupidity is disabled for any work."

96. **Tibetan** reads: "the miserable states of existence" instead of "hell."

30. Mindfulness easily arises for those of good fortune because of their association with a spiritual mentor, and for those who are reverent on account of the instruction of a preceptor and because of their fear.

31. The Buddhas and Bodhisattvas have unobstructed vision in all directions. Everything is in their presence; and I stand in front of them.

32. Meditating thus, one should remain filled with a sense of propriety, respect, and fear; and one should repeatedly think of the Buddhas in this way.

33. When mindfulness stands guard at the gate of the mind, introspection arrives, and once it has come, it does not depart again.[97]

34. First, I should always establish this mind in such a manner, and I should always remain still as if without sense faculties, like a piece of wood.[98]

35. One should never cast one's gaze around without purpose. One should always direct one's gaze downward as if in meditation.

36. However, one should occasionally look around in order to relax the gaze; and if one notices a mere reflection of someone, one should look up to greet him.[99]

37. In order to detect danger on the road and so forth, one should look to the four directions for a moment. Pausing, one should look in the distance, looking behind only after turning around.

38. Upon looking forward or behind, one should go ahead or turn back. Likewise, in all situations one should proceed after realizing what needs to be done.

---

97. **Tibetan:** "...then introspection arrives, and even if it departs, it will return."

98. **Tibetan:** "At times, upon first recognizing that this mind-state is faulty, I should remain still like a piece of wood."

99. **Tibetan:** "... and if someone appears in the field of one's vision, one should look up and give a greeting."

39.   Thinking, "The body should remain like this," and resorting to action again, one should periodically look afresh to see how the body is positioned.

40.   In this way the mad elephant of the mind should be watched diligently so that it is not loosed while tied to the great pillar of the thought of Dharma.

41.   One should examine the mind in this way—where is mine engaged?—so that it does not even for a moment leave the pole of concentration.[100]

42.   If one is unable to do so in the case of danger or a festive occasion, then one should be at ease. It is said that at the time of giving, ethical discipline may be held in abeyance.

43.   Upon recognizing what needs to be undertaken, with a mind focused on that, one should attend to nothing else until one accomplishes it.

44.   For in this way everything is well done. Otherwise neither will occur, and the mental affliction of non-introspection will increase as well.[101]

45.   One should eliminate yearning that arises for various idle conversations, which often take place, and for all kinds of entertainment.

46.   If useless crushing of the earth, ripping of grass, or drawing in the dirt takes place, then fearfully recalling the teaching of the Tathāgata, one should instantly stop it.

47.   When one intends to move or when one intends to speak, one should first examine one's own mind and then act appropriately with composure.

---

100. According to the *Pañjikā*, p. 60, "concentration" *(samādhāna)* refers here to meditative quiescence *(śamatha)*.

   Tibetan: "So that perseverance in concentration is by no means forsaken even for an instant, I should examine the mind thus: Where is my mind engaged?"

101. **Tibetan:** "Thus, everything is well done. Otherwise, neither will occur. In that way, the derivative mental affliction of non-introspection does not increase."

48. When one sees one's own mind to be attached or repulsed, then one should neither act nor speak, but remain still like a piece of wood.

49. When my mind is haughty,[102] sarcastic, full of conceit and arrogance, ridiculing, evasive, and deceitful,

50. When it is inclined to boast, or when it is contemptuous of others, abusive, and irritable, then I should remain still like a piece of wood.

51. When my mind seeks material gain, honor, and fame, or when it seeks attendants and service, then I will remain still like a piece of wood.

52. When my mind is averse to the interests of others and seeks my own self-interest, or when it wishes to speak out of a desire for an audience, then I will remain still like a piece of wood.

53. When it is impatient, indolent, timid, impudent, garrulous, or biased in my own favor, then I will remain still like a piece of wood.

54. Perceiving in this way that the mind is afflicted or engaged in fruitless activities, the hero should always firmly control it by means of an antidote to that.

55. Resolute, confident, steadfast, respectful and courteous, modest, meek, calm, devoted to pleasing others,

56. Undistressed by the mutually incompatible desires of foolish people, endowed with compassion, knowing that they are like this as a consequence of the arising of their mental afflictions,

57. Always resorting to irreproachable things for the sake of myself and others, I will maintain my mind free of pride, like an apparition.

58. Remembering over and over again that after a long time the best of moments of leisure has been obtained, I will keep this mind unshakable, like Sumeru.

---

102. **Tibetan** reads "agitated" *(rgod)* instead of "haughty."

59.   One does not object when the body is being dragged here and there by vultures coveting its flesh. Then why do so now?

60.   Mind, why do you protect this body, appropriating it as your own? If it is really separate from you, what good is it to you?

61.   O fool, if you do not consider as your own a pure wooden statue, why are you guarding this foul machine composed of impurities?

62.   First, with your own intellect, peel off this sheath of skin, and with the knife of wisdom loosen the flesh from the skeleton.

63.   Breaking the bones, look inside at the marrow and examine for yourself, "Where is the essence here?"

64.   If searching carefully in this way, you do not see an essence here, then say why you are still protecting the body today.[103]

65.   If you would not eat it, as impure as it is, and if you would not drink the blood nor suck out the entrails, then what will you do with the body?

66.   However, it is proper to guard it for the sake of feeding the vultures and jackals. This wretched body of humans is an instrument for action.[104]

67.   Even though you protect it so, merciless death will snatch the body away and give it to the vultures.[105] What will you do then?

68.   You do not give clothing and such to a servant if you think he will not stay. The body will eat and pass away. Then why do you waste yourself?[106]

---

103. **Tibetan:** "…then why are you still protecting the body with such attachment?"

104. **Tibetan:** "On the other hand, it is appropriate to guard it for the sake of feeding the vultures and jackals. This human body is just something to be used."

105. **Tibetan:** "…give it to the vultures and dogs."

106. **Tibetan:** "If clothing and so on are not given to a servant who cannot be put to work, since this body departs even though you have fed it, why do you exhaust yourself in caring for it?"

69. Therefore, mind, upon giving the body its wages, now serve your own needs, because not everything earned by a laborer should be given to him.[107]

70. Consider the body as a ship because it is the basis of coming and going. Set the body in motion at your will in order to accomplish the welfare of sentient beings.

71. One who has become self-controlled in that way should always have a smiling face. One should give up frowning and grimacing, be the first to greet, and be a friend to the world.[108]

72. One should not inconsiderately and noisily throw around chairs and the like. One should not pound on the door, and one should always delight in silence.

73. The crane, the cat, or the thief, moving silently and covertly, achieves its desired goal. A sage should always move in such a way.

74. One must respectfully accept the advice of those skilled in directing others and providing unsolicited aid. One should always be the pupil of everyone.

75. One should express one's appreciation for all good words. Having seen someone engaging in virtue, one should cheer him on with praises.

76. One should speak of others' good qualities in their absence and relate them again with satisfaction;[109] and when one's own virtue is discussed, one should consider it as appreciation for good qualities.

---

107. **Tibetan:** "Having given it wages, now make it serve your ends. You should not give everything to something that is of no benefit."

108. **Tibetan:** "...and be a friend of the world and a candid person."

109. **Tibetan:** "One should speak of others' good qualities in their absence and reaffirm those that are mentioned by others."

77.   All endeavors are for the sake of satisfaction, which is difficult to obtain even by means of wealth. So I will enjoy the pleasure of satisfaction in good qualities diligently accomplished by others.[110]

78.   There will be no loss for me in this life, and there will be great happiness in the hereafter. But due to animosities, there is the suffering of aversion and great misery in the hereafter.[111]

79.   In a soft and gentle voice one should speak sincere, coherent words that have clear meaning and are agreeable, pleasant to the ear, and rooted in compassion.[112]

80.   One should always look straight at sentient beings as if drinking them in with the eyes, thinking, "Relying on them alone, I shall attain Buddhahood."[113]

81.   Great blessing arises from continuous yearning for the fields of virtues and kindness, and from an antidote with regard to those who are suffering.[114]

82.   Skillful and vigorous, one should always do the work oneself. With respect to all works, one should not leave the opportunity to someone else.[115]

83.   The perfections of generosity and so forth are progressively more and more lofty. One should not forsake a better one for the sake

---

110. **Tibetan:** "All [Bodhisattva] endeavors bring satisfaction, which is difficult to acquire at any price. So, due to good qualities accomplished for others, I shall experience the joy of satisfaction."

111. **Tibetan:** "...Due to faults, there is the suffering of aversion and great suffering in the hereafter as well."

112. **Tibetan:** "If one is to speak, one should speak sincerely, coherently, with clear meaning, pleasantly, without attachment or hatred, softly, and in moderation."

113. **Tibetan:** "When gazing at sentient beings, one should do so candidly and lovingly, thinking, 'In reliance upon them, I shall attain Buddhahood.'"

114. According to the *Pañjikā*, p. 69, "the field of virtue" is the Buddhas, Bodhisattvas, and so on; "the field of kindness" is one's mother, father, and so on; and an "antidote" is meditation on emptiness (*śūnyatā*), which is an antidote to mental afflictions.

115. **Tibetan:** "Endowed with skill and faith, I should always do the work myself. With respect to all works, I should depend on no one else."

of a lesser, unless it is in accordance with the bridge of the Bodhisattva way of life.[116]

84.   Realizing this, one should always strive for the benefit of others. Even that which is prohibited has been permitted for the compassionate one who foresees benefit.[117]

85.   Sharing with those who have fallen into miserable states of existence, with those who have no protector, and with mendicants, one should eat moderately small portions. Except for the three robes, one should give away everything.

86.   For the sake of an insignificant benefit, one should not harm the body that practices the sublime Dharma, for only in this way can one quickly fulfill the hopes of sentient beings.

87.   Therefore, when the thought of compassion is impure, one should not sacrifice one's life, but it should be sacrificed when one's thought is unbiased. Thus, life must not be wasted.[118]

88.   One should not teach the profound and vast Dharma to the disrespectful, to a healthy person wearing a headdress, to a person with an umbrella, a stick, or a weapon, to one whose head is veiled,

89.   To those who are inadequate,[119] nor to women in the absence of a man. One should pay equal respect to inferior and superior Dharmas.

---

116. The *Pañjikā*, p. 69, explains "the bridge of the Bodhisattva way of life" in the following way: "The Bodhisattvas' way of life, which has the characteristic of guarding the training, is constructed as a bridge to protect the water of virtue."
    Tibetan: "...Do not forsake the greater for the sake of the lesser, and most importantly, consider the welfare of others."

117. **Tibetan:** "...The far-seeing Compassionate One has permitted even that which is forbidden."

118. **Tibetan:** "...but it should be sacrificed as a cause for accomplishing a great purpose for this and other lives."

119. According to the *Pañjikā*, p. 73, the phrase "those who are inadequate" refers to those whose minds are unprepared or to those who are inclined toward the Lesser Vehicle.

90.   One should not expose a vessel of the vast Dharma to an inferior Dharma.[120] Putting aside the Bodhisattva way of life, one should not seduce them with *sūtras* and mantras.

91.   Flagrantly discarding a tooth-stick or spitting is undesirable, and urinating and so forth into water or on land that is usable is contemptible.[121]

92.   One should not eat with a full mouth, noisily, or with the mouth wide open. One should not sit with one's legs outstretched; and one should not rub one's hands together.

93.   One should not travel, lie, or sit alone with someone else's spouse. After observing and inquiring, one should forsake everything that does not please people.[122]

94.   One should not point out anything with one's finger but should respectfully show the way with one's whole right hand.

95.   One should not call out to someone and wave one's arms when there is little urgency; instead, one should snap one's fingers or the like. Otherwise, one would lose composure.[123]

96.   One should lie down in the preferred direction in the lion's posture of the Lord's *nirvāṇa*. One should get up quickly with vigilance and a prior determination.[124]

---

120. According to the *Pañjikā*, p. 73, "a vessel of the vast Dharma" refers to a person fit for receiving the profound and vast Dharma, that is, Mahāyāna; and "inferior Dharma" refers to Śrāvakayāna and other Dharmas.

121. **Tibetan:** "If one discards a tooth-stick or spits, one should cover it up...."

122. **Tibetan:** "...that causes people to lose faith."

123. **Tibetan:** "One should not vigorously wave one's hands but, rather, make a noise by moving them slightly, snapping one's fingers, and so on. Otherwise, one's composure will be lost."

124. **Tibetan:** "One should lie down in the desired direction just as the Lord lay down in *nirvāṇa*, and at the very outset bring forth vigilance and the resolve to rise soon."

97. The conduct of Bodhisattvas is described as immeasurable. One should first surely engage in practices that purify the mind.[125]

98. Three times by day and three times by night one should recite the *Triskandha*.[126] By that means one alleviates the remaining downfalls because of one's reliance on the Jinas and the Spirit of Awakening.

99. One should diligently apply oneself to the trainings that pertain to those situations in which one finds oneself, either of one's own accord or under the influence of others.

100. For there is nothing that the Children of the Jina should not learn. For the good person who behaves in this way, there is nothing that is non-virtuous.[127]

101. One should do nothing other than benefit sentient beings either directly or indirectly; and for the sake of sentient beings alone, one should subordinate everything to Awakening.[128]

102. Never, even at the cost of one's life, should one forsake a spiritual friend who observes the vows of a Bodhisattva and who is well versed in the matters of the Mahāyāna.

103. One should learn from the *Śrīsambhavavimokṣa*[129] respectful behavior toward spiritual mentors. This and other advice of the Buddha should be known through reciting the *sūtras*.

---

125. **Tibetan**: "...One should surely engage to that extent in practices that purify the mind." The Sanskrit *tāvat* could also be translated as "to that extent." However, we have followed here the *Pañjikā*, p. 75, which interprets *tāvat* as *prathamatas*.

126. According to the *Pañjikā*, p. 75, the *Triskandha* is a compilation of the confession of sins *(pāpa-deśanā)*, the rejoicing in virtue *(puṇyānumodana)*, and the ripening of Awakening *(bodhi-pariṇāma)*. rGyal tshab dar ma rin chen's commentary, *sPyod 'jug rnam bshad rgyal sras 'jug ngogs*, 1973, cites the *Triskandha* as the confession of sins *(sdig pa bshags pa)*, the accumulation of merit *(bsod nams gsag pa)*, and methods to prevent virtue from being exhausted and to increase it *(dge ba mi zad cing spel ba'i thabs)*.

127. **Tibetan**: "...For one who is skilled in living in that way, there is nothing that does not become meritorious."

128. **Tibetan**: "...Dedicate everything to enlightenment solely for the sake of sentient beings."

129. The *Śrīsambhavavimokṣa* is a section of the *Āryagaṇḍavyūhasūtra*.

104. The practices are found in the *sūtras*; therefore one should recite them, and one should study the primary downfalls in the *Ākāśagarbhasūtra*.[130]

105. One should definitely study the *Śikṣāsamuccaya*[131] again and again, because good conduct is explained there in detail.

106. Alternatively, one should first look at it briefly, and then carefully read the *Sūtrasamuccaya* composed by Ārya Nāgārjuna.

107. Seeing what is forbidden and what is prescribed, one should implement those teachings for the sake of protecting people's minds.[132]

108. In brief, this alone is the definition of introspection: the repeated examination of the state of one's body and mind.

109. I shall practice it with my body. What is the use of merely reading the words? Will a sick person have any benefit merely by reading about medical treatments?

---

130. **Tibetan:** "...At the very beginning one should examine the *Ākāśagarbhasūtra*."

131. According to Thub bstan chos kyi grags pa, *sPyod 'jug gi 'grel bshad rgyal sras yon tan bum bzang* (mTsho sngon: Krun go'i bod kyi shes rig dpe skrun khang, 1991), p. 318, this refers to the *Śikṣāsamuccaya* composed by Nāgārjuna.

132. **Tibetan:** "One should engage in whatever actions are not forbidden, and in order to protect people's minds, one should observe the teachings and genuinely implement them."

Chapter VI
The Perfection of Patience

1. Anger destroys all the good conduct, such as generosity and worshiping the Sugatas, that has been acquired over thousands of eons.

2. There is no vice like hatred, and there is no austerity like patience. Therefore, one should earnestly cultivate patience in various ways.

3. The mind does not find peace, nor does it enjoy pleasure and joy, nor does it find sleep or fortitude when the thorn of hatred dwells in the heart.

4. Even dependents whom one rewards with wealth and honors wish to harm the master who is repugnant due to his anger.

5. Even friends fear him. He gives, but is not served.[133] In brief, there is nothing that can make an angry person happy.

---

133. **Tibetan:** "He saddens his friends. He attracts with generosity but is not served...."

6. One who recognizes hatred as the enemy, knowing that it creates sufferings such as these, and persistently overcomes it, becomes happy in this world and in the other.[134]

7. Finding its fuel in discontent originating from an undesired event and from an impediment to desired events, anger becomes inflamed and destroys me.

8. Therefore, I shall remove the fuel of that enemy, for that foe has no function other than to harm me.

9. Even if I fall into extreme adversity, I should not disrupt my happiness. When there is frustration, nothing is agreeable, and virtue is forsaken.[135]

10. If there is a remedy, then what is the use of frustration? If there is no remedy, then what is the use of frustration?

11. For loved ones and for oneself, one does not desire suffering, contempt, verbal abuse, or disgrace; but for an enemy, it is the opposite.

12. Happiness is obtained with great difficulty, whereas suffering occurs easily. Only through suffering is there release from the cycle of existence. Therefore, mind, be strong!

13. The devotees of Durgā and the people of Karṇāṭa[136] needlessly endure the pain of burns, cuts, and the like. Why then am I timid when my aim is liberation?

---

134. **Tibetan:** "The enemy, anger, creates such suffering. One who bears down and overcomes it is happy in this and other lives."

135. **Tibetan:** "Whatever happens, I shall not disrupt my cheerfulness. Even if I become frustrated, my desire will not be fulfilled, and my virtue will decline."

136. The *Pañjikā*, p. 84: "The followers of Durgā, that is, the followers of Caṇḍī, upon fasting for three nights or for a day during the ninth day of the bright half of Āśvina, uselessly experience pain while burning, piercing, and cutting their own limbs.... Southerners born in the countries of Karṇāṭa and so forth experience pain and even give up their lives while taking pride in merely writing a name on themselves and competing with each other in many activities."

14. There is nothing whatsoever that remains difficult as one gets used to it.[137] Thus, through habituation with slight pain, even great pain becomes bearable.

15. Do you not consider the pain of bugs, gadflies, and mosquitoes, of thirst and hunger, and the irritation of a serious rash and the like as insignificant?[138]

16. Cold, heat, rain, wind, traveling, illness, captivity, and beatings should not induce a sense of fragility. Otherwise, the distress becomes greater.[139]

17. Some, seeing their own blood, show extraordinary valor, while some faint even at the sight of others' blood.

18. That comes from mental fortitude or from timidity. Therefore, one should become invincible to suffering, and surmount pain.[140]

19. Not even in suffering should a wise person disrupt his mental serenity, for the battle is with the mental afflictions; and in battle pain is easily obtained.[141]

20. Those who conquer the enemy while receiving the enemies' blows on the chest are the victorious heroes. The rest just kill the dead.[142]

---

137. **Tibetan:** "With habituation, there is nothing whatsoever that does not become easier."

138. **Tibetan:** "Why do you not see that the pain of insect and snakebites, or thirst, hunger, and a rash are insignificant?"

139. **Tibetan:** "I should not be impatient with such things as heat, cold, rain, and wind, or with such things as illness, death, and torture. If I am, the pain increases."

140. **Tibetan:** "...Therefore, one should be dismissive of pain and not be overcome by suffering."

141. **Tibetan:** "...and in battle, there is much agony."

142. **Tibetan:** "Courageous victors are dismissive of all suffering, and they conquer such enemies as hatred. The rest just kill corpses."

21.   Suffering has another quality since arrogance diminishes because of despair, and one feels compassion for beings in the cycle of existence, fear of sin, and a yearning for the Jina.[143]

22.   I am not angered at bile and the like even though they cause great suffering. Why be angry at sentient beings, who are also provoked to anger by conditions?[144]

23.   Just as sharp pain arises although one does not desire it, so anger forcibly arises although one does not desire it.[145]

24.   A person does not intentionally become angry, thinking, "I shall get angry," nor does anger originate, thinking, "I shall arise."[146]

25.   All offenses and vices of various kinds arise under the influence of conditions, and they do not arise independently.

26.   An assemblage of conditions does not have the intention, "I shall produce," nor does that which is produced have the intention, "I shall be produced."

27.   That which is regarded as the Primal Substance and that which is construed as the Self do not originate, thinking, "I shall come into being."[147]

28.   Since it has not arisen, how could it wish to come into existence? Since it engages with objects, it cannot strive to cease either.[148]

---

143. **Tibetan:** "Moreover, the advantages of suffering are that despair eliminates arrogance, compassion arises for beings in the cycle of existence, one avoids vice, and one delights in virtue."

144. **Tibetan:** "...Why be angry at those who have minds? They, too, are all impelled by conditions."

145. **Tibetan:** "Just as this illness occurs even though it is unwanted, so do mental afflictions insistently arise even though they are unwanted."

146. **Tibetan:** "Even though they do not think, 'I shall become angry,' people automatically get angry. Likewise, even though it does not think, 'I shall be produced,' anger arises."

147. **Tibetan:** "That which is asserted to be the Primal Substance and that which is designated as the Self do not originate with the intention, 'I shall come into being.'"

148. **Tibetan:** "If they are unborn and do not exist, then why would they wish to come into existence? Since [the Self] always engages with objects, it also cannot cease."

29.   If the permanent Self is not sentient, it is obviously inactive like space. Even in conjunction with conditions, what activity does the immutable have?[149]

30.   What is the use of action to the Self which at the time of action is the same as it was before? If the relationship is that it has action, then which of the two is the cause of the other?[150]

31.   Thus, everything is dependent on something else, and even that on which something is dependent is not autonomous. Hence, why would one get angry at things that are inactive, like apparitions?[151]

32.   [Qualm:] Averting anger is inappropriate, for who averts what? [Response:] That is appropriate, because it is a state of dependent origination and is considered to be the cessation of suffering.[152]

33.   Therefore, upon seeing a friend or an enemy committing a wrong deed, one should reflect, "Such are his conditions," and be at ease.[153]

34.   If all beings would find fulfillment according to their own wishes, then no one would suffer, for no one wishes to suffer.

---

149. **Tibetan:** "If the Self were permanent, it obviously would be inactive like space. Even if it were to come in contact with other influences, what activity would the immutable have?"

150. **Tibetan:** "When it is acted upon, if it remains as it was earlier, what does activity do to it? If it is the activity of [something else], what is the connection [between the Self and the action]?"

151. **Tibetan:** "...Once one knows that, one will not become angry at things, which are all like apparitions."

152. **Tibetan:** [Qualm:] "What counteracts what? Isn't even the counteracting inappropriate?"

[Response:] "There is nothing inappropriate in asserting that miseries are brought to an end in dependence on that."

153. **Tibetan:** "Therefore, if you see an enemy or a friend do something wrong, consider, 'That is due to certain conditions,' and be happy."

35.   People hurt themselves with thorns and the like out of negligence, with fasting and so on out of anger, and by desiring to obtain inaccessible women and so forth.[154]

36.   Some kill themselves by hanging, by jumping from cliffs, by eating poison or unwholesome substances, and by non-virtuous conduct.

37.   When under the influence of mental afflictions, they kill even their own dear selves in this way; then how could they have restraint toward the bodies of others?[155]

38.   If you do not even have compassion toward those who, intoxicated by mental afflictions, commit suicide, then why does anger arise?[156]

39.   If inflicting harm on others is the nature of the foolish, then my anger toward them is as inappropriate as it would be toward fire, which has the nature of burning.

40.   If this fault is adventitious and if sentient beings are good by nature, then anger toward them is inappropriate as it would be toward pungent smoke in the sky.

41.   Disregarding the principal cause, such as a stick and the like, if I become angry with the one who impels it, then it is better if I hate hatred, because that person is also impelled by hatred.

42.   In the past, I too have inflicted such pain on sentient beings; therefore, I, who have caused harm to sentient beings, deserve that in return.

43.   Both his weapon and my body are causes of suffering. He has obtained a weapon, and I have obtained a body. With what should I be angry?

---

154. **Tibetan:** "Due to negligence, they hurt themselves with thorns and so forth, and in order to get women and so on, they become furious and engage in fasting and so on."

155. **Tibetan:** "...then why would they not harm others' bodies?"

156. **Tibetan:** "Even if compassion virtually never arises toward such people who commit suicide and so on due to their mental afflictions, what is the point of getting angry?"

44. Blinded by craving, I have obtained this boil that appears as a human body, which cannot bear to be touched. When there is pain, with whom should one be angry?

45. I do not desire suffering; yet, fool that I am, I desire the cause of suffering. When suffering emerges due to my own fault, why should I be angry with anyone else?

46. Just as the forest of razor-leaves and the birds of hell are brought into existence by my actions, so is this. With whom should I be angry?

47. Those who hurt me are impelled by my actions, as a result of which they will go to the infernal realms. Surely, it is I alone who have ruined them.

48. On account of them, many vices of mine diminish through forbearance. On account of me, they enter the infernal realms with long-lasting agonies.

49. It is I alone who harm them, and they are my benefactors. Wicked mind, why do you misconstrue this and become angry?

50. If there is virtue in my intention, I will not enter the infernal realms. If I protect myself, what will happen to them here?

51. If I were to retaliate, they would not be protected and my conduct would be impaired. Because of that, those in anguish would be lost.

52. Because of its immateriality, the mind can never be harmed by anyone. However, due to its attachment to the body, the mind is tormented by suffering.[157]

53. Neither contempt, abusive speech, nor disgrace harms the body. Why then, mind, do you become angry?

54. Will the unkindness of others toward me devour me in this life or another, that I am so averse to it?[158]

---

157. **Tibetan:** "Because of clinging to the body, the body is harmed by sufferings."

158. **Tibetan:** "Since others' dislike for me will not devour me in this or in other lives, why am I averse to that?"

55. If I am averse to it because it hinders my material gain, my acquisitions will vanish in this life, but my sin will surely remain.

56. It is better that I die today than have a long, corrupt life. For even after living a long time, I shall have the suffering of death.

57. One person wakes up after enjoying a hundred years of pleasure in sleep, and another person wakes up after being happy for a moment.

58. Does happiness return to either once they have awakened? It is the same at the time of death for one who lives a long time and for one who lives a short time.

59. Even though I have acquired many possessions and have enjoyed pleasures for a long time, I shall depart empty-handed and naked as if I had been robbed.

60. What if I destroy vice and perform virtue while living off my acquisitions? Do vice and the destruction of virtue not occur for one who gets angry on account of material gains?[159]

61. If the meaning of my life vanishes, then what is the point of a life that creates only non-virtue?

62. If you think that your hatred toward one who disparages you is because he drives away sentient beings, why does your anger not arise also when others are defamed in the same way?[160]

63. You have patience toward those who are unkind because their ungracious behavior is directed toward someone else, but you do not have patience toward one who disparages you when he is subject to the arising of mental afflictions.[161]

---

159. **Tibetan:** "If one becomes angry on account of one's acquisitions, is merit not exhausted and does vice not arise?"

160. **Tibetan:** [*Qualm:*] "I become angry at disparaging speech, for it drives away sentient beings."

[*Response:*] "Why do you not become angry in the same way at disparaging speech aimed at others?"

161. **Tibetan:** "Since that is due to the others' lack of faith, you are forbearing with regard to that lack of faith. Then since disparaging speech depends on the arising of mental afflictions, why are you not forbearing toward that?"

64. My hatred toward those who revile and violate images, *stūpas*, and the sublime Dharma is wrong, because the Buddhas and the like[162] are free of distress.

65. As in the preceding case, one should ward off anger toward those who injure spiritual mentors, relatives, and friends, by seeing this as arising from conditions.

66. Harm is certainly inflicted on beings either by sentient beings or non-sentient things. This distress is felt in a sentient being, so endure that pain.[163]

67. Some do wrong out of delusion, while others, being deluded, become angry. Among them, whom do we call innocent, and whom do we call guilty?

68. Why did I previously act in such a way that now I am harmed by others? All are subject to their actions. Who am I to alter this?[164]

69. Realizing this, I shall strive for virtues in such a way that all will have loving thoughts toward each other.

70. When fire spreads from one burning house to another, one should bundle up the straw and the like, take it out, and discard it.

71. Likewise, when the mind burns with the fire of hatred due to attachment, one should immediately cast it aside because of the fear of burning the body of merit.

72. If one who is to be executed has a hand amputated and is released, is this unfortunate? If a person is freed from hell by human suffering, is this unfortunate?

---

162. According to the *Pañjikā*, p. 97, the phrase "and so on" implies the Bodhisattvas, noble Śrāvakas, and Pratyekabuddhas.

163. **Tibetan:** "Why do you especially rage at those who are sentient? Therefore, endure that harm."

164. **Tibetan:** "...Why then do I become furious at this?"

73. If one is unable to endure even this slight suffering of the present, then why does one not ward off anger which is the cause of pain in hell?

74. Thus, solely due to anger I have brought myself into hells thousands of times, and I have not brought about benefit for myself or others.[165]

75. But this suffering is not of that kind, and it will bring about great benefit. Only delight in suffering that eliminates the suffering of the world is appropriate here.

76. If others find pleasure and joy in praising the abundance of someone's good qualities, why, mind, do you not praise it and delight in this way, too?

77. This joy from your rejoicing is a blameless source of happiness. It is not prohibited by the virtuous ones, and it is the most excellent way to attract others.

78. If you do not like it, thinking that it is a pleasure for that person only, then if you were to stop giving wages and the like, your seen and unseen reward would be destroyed.[166]

79. When your own good qualities are being praised, you want others to rejoice as well. When good qualities of someone else are being praised, you do not want happiness even for yourself.

80. Upon generating the Spirit of Awakening out of the desire for the happiness of all sentient beings, why are you angry at sentient beings now that they have found happiness themselves?

81. If you desire sentient beings' Buddhahood, which is worshiped in the three worlds, then why are you burned up when you see them slightly honored?

---

165. **Tibetan:** "On account of sensual desires I have experienced burning and so on in hell thousands of times, but I have not accomplished either my own or others' welfare."

166. **Tibetan:** "Moreover, if you do not desire the joy [of thinking], 'He is happy,' due to refusing to grant wages and so forth, you will fail in terms of the seen and the unseen." In this verse the phrase "the seen and the unseen" refers to this and future lifetimes.

82. One who nurtures a person whom you should nurture is making you a gift. Upon finding a person who supports your family, are you not delighted, but angry?[167]

83. What does one who wishes Awakening for sentient beings not wish for them? How can one who becomes angry at others' prosperity have the Spirit of Awakening?

84. If someone does not receive that gift and if it remains in the house of the benefactor, then you do not have it anyway. So what use is it to you, whether it is given away or not?

85. Why would you have him ward off merits, kind people, and his own good qualities? Let him not accept when he is being given something? Say, at what are you angry?

86. Not only do you not repent for sins you have committed, but you also wish to compete with others who have performed virtues.

87. If something unpleasant happens to your enemy, would your satisfaction make it happen again? It would not happen merely due to your desire, without a cause.[168]

88. Even if it is brought about by your desire, would you find happiness in his suffering? Even if there were advantage in it for you, what other disadvantage would come out of it?[169]

89. For this horrible fishhook is cast by the fishermen, the mental afflictions, from whom the guardians of hells will buy you and will stew you in infernal cauldrons.[170]

---

167. **Tibetan:** "If a friend takes care of someone you are supposed to serve, instead of being pleased, do you become angry again?"

168. **Tibetan:** "Even if your enemy is unhappy, what is the point of your satisfaction in that? Your mere desire will not cause him harm."

169. **Tibetan:** "Even if that suffering were brought about by your desire, why would you take delight in that? If you say it brings you satisfaction, what is worse than that?"

170. **Tibetan:** "Once I am snagged by this horrible fishhook cast by the fishermen, the mental afflictions, I will certainly be stewed in infernal cauldrons by the guardians of hell."

90. Praise, fame, and honor are not conducive to my merit, long life, strength, health, or physical well-being.

91. The wise person who knows what is best for himself would find benefit in these. One desiring mental happiness would pursue drinking, gambling, and the like.[171]

92. For the sake of fame, some sacrifice their wealth and even kill themselves. Can words be eaten? And when one dies, who feels that pleasure?[172]

93. At the loss of praise and fame, my own mind appears to me just like a child who wails in distress when its sand castle is destroyed.

94. Since a word is not sentient, it cannot praise me. But knowing that someone likes me is a cause of my delight.

95. Whether it is for someone else or for me, what good to me is the affection of another? That joy of affection belongs only to that person. Not even a tiny fraction of that belongs to me.

96. If I take pleasure in that person's pleasure, then I should take it in every single case. Why am I unhappy when others are made happy through their favor for someone else?

97. Therefore, it is because I am being praised that pleasure arises in me. But due to such absurdity, this is nothing more than the behavior of a child.

98. Praise and so forth obliterate my peace and disillusionment with the cycle of existence.[173] They stir up jealousy toward gifted people, and anger at their success.

99. Therefore, are those conspiring to destroy my reputation and so forth not protecting me from falling into hell?[174]

---

171. **Tibetan:** "If I recognize my own self-interest, what good is there in that for me? If I want only mental pleasure, I should devote myself to gambling, drinking, and so on."

172. **Tibetan:** "For the sake of fame, some sacrifice their wealth and even kill themselves. Yet what good are words? When one dies, who has that pleasure?"

173. **Tibetan**: "Praise and so on distract me and remove my disillusionment [with the cycle of existence]."

100. The bondage of acquisition and honor is unfitting for me who seeks liberation. How can I hate those who are freeing me from bondage?

101. How can I hate those who, as if due to the Buddha's blessing, block the gate as I seek to enter suffering?

102. It is wrong to feel anger toward someone, thinking that person impedes my merit. As there is no austerity equal to patience, shall I not abide in that?

103. If on account of my own fault I do not practice patience here, then I myself have created an obstacle when grounds for merit have been presented.

104. If one thing does not exist without another, and does exist when the other is present, then that other thing is its cause. How can that be called a hindrance?

105. For a supplicant is not a hindrance to generosity at the time of almsgiving; and when a person who bestows an ordination arrives, he is not called a hindrance to the ordination.

106. Beggars are easy to meet in the world, but malefactors are difficult to find, for no one will wrong me when I do no wrong.[175]

107. Therefore, since my adversary assists me in my Bodhisattva way of life, I should long for him like a treasure discovered in the house and acquired without effort.

108. Thus, he and I have obtained this fruit of patience. It should be given to him first, for patience is caused by him.

109. If an adversary does not deserve respect because his intention was not that I accomplish patience, then why is the sublime Dharma honored? It too has no intention to be a cause of that achievement.

---

174. **Tibetan:** "Therefore, are those who stand against me to destroy my reputation and so on not actually protecting me from falling into the miserable states of existence?"

175. This statement refers to the karmic consequences of actions from one life to another, namely, that one will be injured by others only if one has harmed others in the past. This is not to say, of course, that one may not be harmed by others whom one has not hurt in this life.

110. If an adversary is not respected because his intention is to cause harm, then for what other reason would I have patience toward him, if he is like a physician who is intent on my well-being?

111. Thus, patience arises only in dependence on that malicious intention, so he alone is a cause of my patience. I should respect him just like the sublime Dharma.

112. The Sage has declared that the field of sentient beings is the field of the Jinas, because many have reached the highest fulfillment by honoring them.

113. As the attainment of the Buddha's qualities is equally due to sentient beings and to the Jinas, how is it that I do not respect sentient beings as I do the Jinas?

114. Their greatness is not in terms of their intention but in terms of the result itself. The greatness of sentient beings is comparable to that, so they are equal.

115. A friendly disposition, which is honorable, is the very greatness of sentient beings. The merit due to faith in the Buddhas is the very greatness of the Buddhas.

116. Therefore, sentient beings are equal to the Jinas in their share in the acquisition of the qualities of the Buddha; but none of them are equal to the Buddhas, who are oceans of good qualities with endless portions.

117. If even a minute good quality of those who are a unique collection of the essence of good qualities is found in someone, not even the three worlds would be enough to honor that one.

118. Sentient beings have the best portion of emerging qualities of a Buddha. One should honor sentient beings in accordance with that share.[176]

119. Apart from respecting sentient beings, what other repayment to true friends, the immeasurable benefactors, is possible?

---

176. **Tibetan:** "Because sentient beings have some portion of the superb qualities of the Buddha, it is right to honor sentient beings for just that similarity."

120. One should render only service to those for whose sake they cut apart their bodies and enter the Avici hell. Therefore, one should treat people kindly even though they inflict great harm.[177]

121. Why do I generate pride and not act like a servant toward those masters for whose sake my Lords have no regard for their own selves?

122. By pleasing those in whose happiness the Lords of Sages find delight and in whose pain they experience grief, all the Lords of Sages are gratified; and to wrong them is to wrong the Sages.[178]

123. Just as there is no mental pleasure in all sensual gratification whatsoever when one's body is on fire, likewise there is no way for the Compassionate Ones to be happy when sentient beings are in pain.

124. Therefore, whatever pain I have brought to all those of great compassion by harming sentient beings, that sin I now confess. May the Sages forgive that which has aggrieved them.[179]

125. In order to please the Tathāgatas, today with my entire being I place myself in the service of the world. Let streams of people step on my head and strike me down. May the Protector of the World be pleased.

126. There is no doubt whatsoever that those Compassionate Beings regard all beings as themselves. Are they not seen as the Protectors in the form of sentient beings? Why then is there disrespect for them?

---

177. **Tibetan:** "[The kindness of the Bodhisattvas], who sacrifice their lives and enter Avici, is repaid by service [to sentient beings], so even if [sentient beings] harm one, they are all to be treated with kindness."

178. **Tibetan:** "The Sages are delighted with their joy, and they are not pleased if they are harmed; by pleasing them, all the Sages are overjoyed, and to injure them is to injure the Sages."

179. **Tibetan:** "Therefore, whatever displeasure I have brought to all the great Compassionate Ones by harming sentient beings, I confess that sin today. Thus, may I be forgiven by the Sages whom I have displeased."

127. This alone[180] is pleasing to the Tathāgatas. This alone is the accomplishment of one's own goal. This alone removes the suffering of the world. Therefore, let this alone be my resolve.

128. When some king's man tyrannizes the populace, the farsighted among them cannot retaliate,

129. Because that man is not alone and his power is the king's power.[181] So one should not disparage any weak person who has done wrong,

130. Since his power is the guardians of hell and the Compassionate Ones. Therefore, one should please sentient beings, just as a servant would a hot-tempered king.

131. What could an angry king do that would equal the anguish of hell, experienced as a result of inflicting mental pain on sentient beings?

132. What could a gratified king give that would equal Buddhahood, experienced as a result of delighting sentient beings?

133. Let alone future Buddhahood, do you not see that in this life, fortune, fame, and happiness ensue from pleasing sentient beings?

134. While transmigrating, a patient person attains beauty, health, charisma, long life, and the abundant joy of a Cakravarti.[182]

---

180. According to the *Pañjikā*, p. 114, "this alone" refers to one's service to sentient beings (*sattvārādhana*).

181. **Tibetan:** "Although some king's man torments the populace, the farsighted among them do not retaliate even though they are able, for he is not alone and his power is the king's power."

182. **Tibetan:** "While transmigrating, a patient person, with beauty, health, charisma, and so forth, achieves longevity and the abundant joy of a Cakravarti."

Chapter VII
The Perfection of Zeal

1. Thus, one who has patience should cultivate zeal, because Awakening is established with zeal, and there is no merit without zeal, just as there is no movement without wind.

2. What is zeal? It is enthusiasm for virtue. What is said to be its antithesis? It is spiritual sloth, clinging to the reprehensible, apathy, and self-contempt.

3. Spiritual sloth arises from indolence, indulging in pleasures, sleep, and craving for lounging around due to one's apathy toward the miseries of the cycle of existence.

4. Scented out by the hunters, the mental afflictions, you have entered the snare of rebirth. Why do you not recognize even now that you are in the mouth of death?

5. You do not see that those of your own kind are gradually being killed. You even fall asleep like a buffalo among butchers.

6. When Yama watches you and your path is blocked on all sides, how can you enjoy eating, and how can you sleep and have sexual intercourse?

7. Since death will come swiftly, with its implements prepared, what will you do then even if you have abandoned spiritual sloth at this wrong time?[183]

8. Thinking: "I have not achieved this. I have just started this, but it remains half-done. Death has suddenly arrived. Oh, I am wretched,"

9. Seeing despondent relatives with their eyes swollen and red, with tears on their faces from the impact of their grief and the faces of the messengers of Yama,

10. Tormented by the recollection of your own vices, hearing the sounds of hell, and befouling your body with excrement out of fear, what will you do when you are so terrified?

11. Realizing "I am like a live fish," your fear is appropriate now. How much more when you have committed vices and face the intense suffering of hell?

12. So, delicate one, you burn even when touched by hot water. Upon performing deeds leading to hell, how will you remain at ease?

13. You expect results with no effort. So delicate you are and in so much pain. While in the clutches of death, you act like an immortal. Hey, miserable one, you are destroying yourself![184]

14. Upon finding the boat of human birth now, cross the great river of suffering. O fool, there is no time for sleep, for this boat is hard to catch again.

15. Forsaking the supreme joy of Dharma, which is an endless stream of joy, how can you delight in frivolity and jokes, which are two causes of suffering?[185]

---

183. **Tibetan:** "Since death will come swiftly, until it does, one should accumulate the collections [of merit and knowledge]. Even if one rejects spiritual sloth at the time [of death], what will you do at this wrong time?"

184. **Tibetan:** "...Alas, you are destroyed by miseries!"

185. **Tibetan:** "Having forsaken the supreme joy of Dharma, which is the cause of endless joy, due to causes of suffering do you take delight in distractions, jokes, and the like?"

16.   The absence of apathy, the array of abilities such as prudence, self-control, equality between oneself and others, and exchange of oneself for others

17.   Should be practiced without the discouragement of thinking, "How could I possibly attain Awakening?" For the truth-speaking Tathāgata proclaimed this truth:

18.   "Even those who were gadflies, mosquitoes, bees, and worms attained supreme Awakening, which is difficult to attain, through the power of their effort."

19.   Human by birth and capable of knowing what is beneficial and what is not, why could I not attain Awakening as long as I do not forsake the guidance of the Omniscient One?[186]

20.   If I fear, thinking, "I shall have to sacrifice my arms, legs, and the like," I may confuse the important with the insignificant due to my lack of discrimination.[187]

21.   For countless millions of eons I shall be cut, pierced, burned, and split open many times, but Awakening will not occur.

22.   However, this limited suffering of mine, which yields perfect Awakening, is like the suffering of extraction when removing the pain of an embedded splinter.[188]

23.   All physicians cure with unpleasant treatments. Therefore, to destroy a multitude of pains, a slight one must be endured.

---

186. **Tibetan:** "Human by birth and recognizing what is beneficial and what is harmful, if one such as myself were not to abandon the conduct of enlightenment, why could I not achieve enlightenment?"

187. **Tibetan:** "If I think, 'I shall have to sacrifice my arms and legs,' my fear is due to confusion, without discriminating between what is important and what is insignificant."

188. **Tibetan:** "This suffering of mine that induces enlightenment is limited. It is like the suffering of an incision made in order to remove the harm of a debilitating disease."

24.   Although such treatment is customary, the Supreme Physician does not give it. He cures chronic diseases with gentle treatment.[189]

25.   At the beginning, the Guide prescribes giving vegetables and the like. One does it gradually so that later one can give away even one's own flesh.[190]

26.   When insight arises that one's own flesh is like a vegetable, then what difficulty is there in giving away one's flesh and bone?[191]

27.   On account of abandoing vices, one does not suffer, and on account of being wise, one does not become troubled in mind; for mental pain is due to false conceptions, and bodily pain is due to sinful actions.

28.   The body is well on account of merit; and the mind is joyful on account of wisdom. What can afflict a compassionate one who stays in the cycle of existence for the sake of others?

29.   Extinguishing previous vices and accumulating oceans of merit, owing to the power of the Spirit of Awakening alone, one moves ahead of the Śrāvakas.

30.   Upon mounting the chariot of the Spirit of Awakening, which carries away all despondency and weariness, what sensible person would despair at progressing in this way from joy to joy?[192]

31.   The powers of aspiration, steadfastness, delight, and letting go are for the sake of accomplishing the benefit of sentient beings. Out of fear of suffering, one should generate that aspiration as one contemplates its blessings.

---

189. **Tibetan:** "Such ordinary treatment is not rendered by the Supreme Physician. Rather, by very gentle means, he heals immeasurable, chronic diseases."

190. **Tibetan:** "The Guide encourages us at the beginning to give vegetables and so on. Once we are accustomed to that, then later on we can gradually give away even our own flesh."

191. **Tibetan:** "When there arises the attitude of regarding one's own body as being like a vegetable and so forth, what problem is there in giving away one's own flesh?"

192. **Tibetan:** "Thus, while mounted on the steed of the Spirit of Awakening, which banishes all despondency and weariness, as one moves from joy to joy, what sensible person would despair?"

32. Uprooting its opposite in this way, one should strive to increase one's zeal with the powers of aspiration, self-confidence, delight, letting go, dedication, and determination.

33. I must eliminate immeasurable faults for myself and for others. While the eradication of every single fault may take myriads of eons,

34. There I do not see even a small fraction of a beginning of the elimination of faults. Why does my heart not burst open when I am to be allotted immeasurable suffering?[193]

35. I must acquire many good qualities for myself and for others; otherwise, the cultivation of every single good quality may not take place in myriads of eons.[194]

36. I have never trained in even a small fraction of good qualities. It is astonishing that this life, which I have somehow obtained, has been spent in vain.

37. I have not found joy in great festivals and offerings to the Blessed One. I have not paid my respect to the teaching, nor have I fulfilled the hopes of the poor.[195]

38. I have not granted fearlessness to the frightened, nor have I comforted the distressed. I became a spear in the womb just for my mother to suffer.[196]

---

193. **Tibetan:** "I shall eliminate my own and others' immeasurable faults. While it takes oceans of eons to eliminate each of those faults, if I do not see even a fraction of a beginning of the elimination of faults, why does my heart not burst, as I am a locus of immeasurable suffering?"

194. **Tibetan:** vv. 35-36. "I shall bring about a multitude of excellent qualities of myself and others. While each good quality is to be cultivated for oceans of eons, I have never cultivated even a fraction of excellence. It is appalling that this life, which I have somehow obtained, has been lived in vain."

195. **Tibetan:** "I have not worshiped the Blessed One, nor have I provided the joy of great festivals. I have not implemented the teaching, nor have I fulfilled the hopes of the poor."

196. **Tibetan:** "...I have just created pain and suffering in my mother's womb."

39. Due to my former lack of aspiration for Dharma, such a disaster has befallen me now. Who would forsake the aspiration for Dharma?

40. The Sage declared that aspiration is a root of all virtues, and the root of that is constantly meditating on the results of the maturation of *karma*.

41. Miseries, depressions, various fears, and impediments to their desires befall those who do evil.[197]

42. Wherever the heart's desire of those who perform virtue goes, there its own merits honor it with an offering of its results.[198]

43. But wherever the desire for happiness of the evil-doers goes, there vices destroy it with weapons of sufferings.[199]

44. On account of their virtues, the Children of the Sugata, who dwell in the hearts of spacious, fragrant, and cool lotuses, whose splendor is enhanced with the nourishment of the sweet voice of the Jina, and whose handsome bodies emerge from the lotuses blossomed by the rays of the Sage, are born in the presence of the Sugata.[200]

45. On account of non-virtues, one cries out in distress, one's entire skin is ripped away by the agents of Yama, one's body is immersed into copper melted by the heat of fire, pieces of one's flesh are cut off by hundreds of strokes of blazing spears and swords, and one repeatedly falls on intensely heated iron grounds.

---

197. **Tibetan:** "Suffering, misery, various fears, and separation from the desired occur due to committing sin."

198. **Tibetan:** "By performing an intended virtue, wherever one goes, one will be honored with the resultant benefits of one's merit."

199. **Tibetan:** "Although a sinner desires happiness, wherever he goes, sin destroys [his happiness] with the weapons of suffering."

200. According to the *Pañjikā*, p. 127, "in the presence of the Sugata" means in the presence of the Bhagavān Amitābha in Sukhāvatī.

    Tibetan: "Due to virtues, the Children of Sugatas, who dwell in the hearts of spacious, fragrant, cool lotuses, whose splendor is enhanced with the nourishment of the sweet voices of the Jinas, and whose superb bodies emerge from lotuses that are opened by the light of the Sages, remain in the presence of the Jinas."

46. Therefore, one should nurture an aspiration for virtue, cultivating it with reverence. Once one has begun, one should cultivate self-confidence according to the method discussed in the *Vajradhvajasūtra.*[201]

47. After first examining one's means, one should either begin or not begin. Surely, it is better not to begin than to turn back once one has begun.[202]

48. This habit continues even in another life; and due to that sin, suffering increases. Another opportunity for action is lost, and the task is not accomplished.[203]

49. One should apply self-confidence to these three: actions, secondary mental afflictions,[204] and ability. "I alone should do it" expresses self-confidence with regard to action.

50. This world overwhelmed by mental afflictions is incapable of accomplishing its own self-interest. Therefore, I must do it for them. I am not as incapable as the world is.[205]

51. Why should someone else do inferior work while I stand by? If I do not do it because of pride, then it is better to let my pride be destroyed.

---

201. **Tibetan:** "Therefore, aspire for virtue, and cultivate it with reverence. Once one has begun, one should cultivate self-confidence with the aid of the *Vajradhvajasūtra.*"

202. **Tibetan:** "After examining a project at the beginning, either initiate it or do not initiate it. It is better not to initiate it than to begin it and then turn back."

203. **Tibetan:** "Otherwise one will be habituated to that in other lifetimes, and sin and suffering will increase; for the time of other [activities] and their results will be postponed and will not be accomplished."

204. The *Pañjikā*, p. 128, indicates that secondary mental afflictions refer here either to seven mental afflictions, beginning with anger (*krodha*), malice (*upanāha*), disparagement (*mrakṣa*), envious rivalry (*pradāśa*), and so on or to fifty mental afflictions beginning with attachment (*rāga*) and so on.

205. **Tibetan:** "The world, overwhelmed by mental afflictions, is incapable of accomplishing its own self-interest. Thus, since beings are not as capable as myself, I shall do this."

52.   Even a crow behaves like a *garuḍa* when attacking a dead water snake. If my mind is weak, even a small adversity is troubling.[206]

53.   When one is made powerless by despondency, adversities are easily caused, but one who is uplifted and zealous is invincible even in the face of great adversities.[207]

54.   Therefore, with an unswerving mind, I shall bring disaster to adversity. For as long as I am conquered by adversities, my desire for victory over the three worlds is ludicrous.[208]

55.   I should overcome everything and not be overcome by anything. I should acquire this self-confidence, for I am a Child of the Lions, the Jinas.[209]

56.   Beings who are overcome by pride are wretched and not self-confident; they are under the power of the enemy, pride. A self-confident person does not succumb to the power of the enemy.

57.   Led by pride to miserable states of existence, they are devoid of joy even in human life. They are slaves who eat others' morsels, stupid, ugly, and feeble.

58.   They are despised everywhere, puffed up with pride, and miserable. If they are included among the self-confident, they are pitiable. Say, of what kind are they?[210]

---

206. **Tibetan:** "...When I am frail, even a small adversity hurts."

207. **Tibetan:** "In the case of despondency and apathy, what liberation is there from this impoverishment? If effort is generated with self-confidence, it is difficult to be overpowered by even great [adversities]."

208. **Tibetan:** "Therefore, with an indomitable attitude I shall overcome all adversities. If I am overwhelmed by adversities, my desire for victory over the three worlds will be ludicrous."

209. **Tibetan:** "I shall gain victory over everything, and no one will be victorious over me. As a Child of the Lions, the Jinas, I shall dwell in this self-confidence."

210. **Tibetan:** "Inflated with afflictive pride, pride leads them to miserable states of existence, and it spoils the celebration of human life. They will become slaves who eat others' morsels, stupid, ugly, pathetic, and despised everywhere. If ascetics inflated with pride are also included among the self-confident, tell me: Who else is so pitiable?"

59.   They are self-confident and victorious heroes who bear their self-confidence in order to conquer the enemy, pride. Upon killing that growing enemy, pride, they demonstrate the fruit of their victory to the world as they please.

60.   Abiding amidst a multitude of mental afflictions, one should be vigorous in a thousand ways and unconquerable by the hosts of mental afflictions, like a lion by a herd of deer.[211]

61.   Even in great troubles, the eye does not perceive flavor.[212] Likewise, upon encountering difficulty, one should not be overcome by mental afflictions.[213]

62.   One should diligently apply oneself to the action in which one engages. Intoxicated by that action, one should be of an insatiable mind, like one striving for the satisfaction of the result of a game.[214]

63.   An action is performed for the sake of happiness, and yet happiness may or may not occur. But how can one who delights in action itself be happy when inactive?[215]

---

211. **Tibetan:** "When I dwell in the midst of mental afflictions, I shall stand up to them in a thousand ways. Like a lion among jackals and so on, I shall not be conquered by the multitude of mental afflictions."

212. According to the *Pañjikā*, p. 131, sweet and other types of flavors, which should be apprehended by the tongue.

213. **Tibetan:** "Even in the event of great troubles, people protect their eyes. Likewise, in times of difficulties, I shall not submit to mental afflictions." Following this verse, the Tibetan version includes the following stanza: "Let me be burned to death or beheaded, but never shall I bow in any way to my enemies, the mental afflictions. Likewise, in all situations I shall do nothing that is not appropriate."

214. According to the *Pañjikā*, p. 131, "a game" refers to the game of dice, that is, gambling and so forth.
      Tibetan: "Like one who yearns for the joyful results of a game, I shall long for whatever task is at hand; and I shall pursue the task with insatiable delight."

215. **Tibetan:** "Although one performs an action for the sake of happiness, there is no guarantee as to whether or not happiness will ensue. But how can one whose action is joyful be happy when not performing that action?"

64.   In the cycle of existence, there is no satisfaction in sensual desires, which are like honey on a razor's edge. How can there be satiation with the nectar of merits, which are sweet in their maturation and beneficial?[216]

65.   Therefore, even upon the completion of an action, one should immerse oneself in it again, just as an elephant, scorched by the midday sun, immediately approaches a lake.[217]

66.   And when one's strength begins to decline, one should quit so that one can re-engage later. When a task has been well completed, one should leave it with the desire for more and more.[218]

67.   One should ward off the blows of mental afflictions and severely attack them, as if engaged in a sword-combat with a trained enemy.[219]

68.   Just like one would quickly, fearfully pick up a dropped sword, so should one pick up the dropped sword of mindfulness, while bearing the hells in mind.[220]

69.   Just as poison spreads throughout the body once it has reached the blood, so does a fault spread throughout the mind once it has reached a vulnerable spot.[221]

---

216. **Tibetan:** "Like honey on a razor's edge, sensual desires provide no satisfaction. How then can one be satiated with merit, which ripens as joy and peace?"

217. **Tibetan:** "Therefore, in order to complete a task, engage in it again, just as an elephant scorched by the midday sun comes to a lake and plunges in."

218. **Tibetan:** "When one's strength is about to wane, one should discontinue it so that one can get back to it again; and when a task has been well completed, one should leave it with the desire for more and more."

219. **Tibetan:** "Like engaging in a fencing duel with a seasoned enemy, one should avoid the weapons of the mental afflictions and gently bind these enemies, the mental afflictions."

220. **Tibetan:** "If one drops one's sword while in battle, out of fear one swiftly picks it up. Likewise, if one loses the weapon of mindfulness, one should retrieve it quickly, bearing in mind the fear of hell."

221. **Tibetan:** "Just as poison spreads throughout the body in dependence upon [the arteries], so does a fault spread in the mind when it gets the opportunity."

70. A practitioner should be like someone carrying a jar of oil while under the scrutiny of swordsmen, careful of stumbling out of fear of death.[222]

71. Therefore, just as one quickly jumps up when a snake creeps onto one's lap, so should one swiftly counteract the advent of drowsiness and sloth.

72. At every single disgrace, one should burn with remorse and ponder: "How shall I act so that this does not happen to me again?"

73. One should seek for companionship or for an appointed task with this motive: "How may I practice mindfulness in these circumstances?"[223]

74. Bringing to mind the teaching on conscientiousness, one should arouse oneself so that one is always prepared before encountering a task.[224]

75. Just as cotton is swayed in the direction of the wind's coming and going, so should one surrender oneself to one's enthusiasm, and in this way one's supernormal powers will thrive.[225]

---

222. **Tibetan:** "A practitioner should concentrate like a frightened person carrying a jar of mustard oil while being scrutinized by someone holding a sword who threatens him with death if he spills it."

223. **Tibetan:** "With that motive, one should seek to meet [with spiritual mentors] or engage in appropriate actions."

224. **Tibetan:** "Before engaging in an action, one should be prepared for everything. Thus, bearing in mind the advice on conscientiousness, one should rise to the task."

225. According to the *Pañjikā*, p.135, "supernormal powers" (*ṛddhi*) refer to sky-walking and so on.
    Tibetan: "Just as cotton moves under the influence of the going and coming of the wind, so should one surrender to enthusiasm, in which case one will meet with success."

Chapter VIII
The Perfection of Meditation

1. Upon developing zeal in that way, one should stabilize the mind in meditative concentration, since a person whose mind is distracted lives between the fangs of mental afflictions.

2. With bodily and mental seclusion, distraction does not arise. Therefore, upon renouncing the world, one should renounce discursive thoughts.

3. On account of attachment and craving for gain and the like, one does not renounce the world. Thus, upon forsaking them, the wise should contemplate in this way.

4. Realizing that one who is well endowed with insight through quiescence[226] eradicates mental afflictions, one should first seek quiescence. Quiescence is due to detachment toward the world and due to joy.[227]

---

226. Insight *(vipaśyanā)* is defined in the *Pañjikā*, p. 137, as "wisdom *(prajñā)* that has the nature of thorough knowledge of reality as it is." Quiescence *(śamatha)* is defined as "meditative concentration *(samādhi)* that has the characteristic of mental single-pointedness *(cittaikāgratā)*."

227. **Tibetan:** "Recognizing that the mental afflictions are eradicated by insight imbued with quiescence, one should first seek quiescence. That is achieved with detachment toward the world and with joy."

5.   For what impermanent person, who will not see his loved ones again in thousands of births, is it appropriate to be attached to impermanent beings?[228]

6.   Failing to see them, one does not find joy nor does one abide in meditative concentration. Even upon seeing them, one does not become satisfied but is tormented by strong desire, just as before.[229]

7.   One does not perceive reality and loses disillusionment with the cycle of existence. One is consumed by that grief—desire for the company of the beloved.[230]

8.   Because of thinking of that person, life ever so swiftly passes in vain. Due to a transient entity, the eternal Dharma is lost.[231]

9.   One who acts in the same manner as foolish people definitely goes to a miserable state of existence. They do not like someone who is different. What is gained from association with fools?[232]

10.   One moment they are friends, and the next moment they are enemies. On an occasion for being pleased, they become angry. Ordinary people[233] are difficult to gratify.

11.   When given good advice, they become angry; and they turn me away from good advice. If they are not listened to, they become angry and go to a miserable state of existence.

---

228. **Tibetan:** "No impermanent person who has attachment for impermanent people will see his loved ones again for a thousand lifetimes."

229. **Tibetan:** "If one does not see them, one becomes unhappy, and the mind does not reach meditative equipoise. Even if they are seen, there is no satisfaction, so one is again tormented by craving just as before."

230. **Tibetan:** "If one is attached to sentient beings, reality is obscured, one's disillusionment [with the cycle of existence] is obliterated, and in the end one is consumed by grief."

231. **Tibetan:** "Solely due to thinking of them, this life passes by in vain. Even the eternal Dharma is lost due to transient friends."

232. **Tibetan:** "If one behaves like foolish people, one will certainly go to a miserable state of existence. If one is led to [conduct] dissimilar to [that of the wise], what is the point of associating with fools?"

233. According to the *Pañjikā*, p. 138, ordinary people *(pṛthag-jana)* are those who are not *āryas*, that is, those have not gained the direct realization of identitylessness.

12. They feel envy toward a superior, competitiveness with a peer, arrogance toward one who is inferior, conceit due to praise, and anger due to reproach. When could there be any benefit from a fool?[234]

13. Between one fool and another, something non-virtuous is inevitable, such as glorification of one's own self, speaking ill of others, and conversation about the pleasures of the cycle of existence.[235]

14. Thus, on account of one's association with someone else, one encounters adversity. I shall happily live alone with a non-afflicted mind.[236]

15. One should flee far from a fool. One should gratify the encountered person with pleasantries, not with the intention of intimacy, but in the manner of a kind and impartial person.[237]

16. Taking only what benefits Dharma, like a bee taking nectar from a flower, I shall live everywhere without acquaintance, as if I had not existed before.

17. A mortal who thinks, "I am rich and respected, and many like me," experiences fear of approaching death.[238]

18. Wherever the mind, infatuated by pleasures, finds enjoyment, there a thousandfold suffering arises and falls to one's share.[239]

---

234. **Tibetan:** "They become jealous of their superiors, competitive with their peers, and arrogant toward their subordinates. If they are praised, they become conceited, and if they are disparaged, they respond with anger. When is benefit ever gained from the foolish?"

235. **Tibetan:** "If one accompanies the foolish, with regard to [other] fools, one praises oneself and disparages others; and non-virtues, such as speaking of the pleasures of the cycle of existence, certainly arise."

236. **Tibetan:** "Thus, that association between myself and others simply leads to ruin. They do not fulfill my needs, nor do I fulfill theirs."

237. **Tibetan:** "Therefore, I shall flee far away from the foolish. If I encounter them, I shall greet them pleasantly, but without becoming intimate with them, I shall casually act with propriety."

238. **Tibetan:** "If one has the arrogance of thinking, 'I have wealth and honor, and I am loved by many,' fear will arise following death."

239. **Tibetan:** "Thus, in conjunction with every object of attachment of the infatuated mind, suffering arises a thousand times."

19.   Hence, the wise should not desire it. Fear arises from desire, yet it passes away by itself. Generate fortitude and look at it with indifference.[240]

20.   Many have become wealthy and many have become famous, but no one knows where they have gone with their wealth and fame.

21.   If others despise me, why should I rejoice when praised? If others praise me, why should I be despondent when reviled?

22.   If sentient beings of different dispositions have not been satisfied by the Jinas themselves, then how could they be by an ignorant person like myself? So, what is the point of attending to the world?

23.   They revile a person without acquisitions and despise a person with acquisitions. How can those whose company is by nature suffering bring forth joy?

24.   The Tathāgatas have said that a fool is no one's friend, because the affection of a fool does not arise without self-interest.

25.   Love due to self-interest is love for one's own sake, just as distress at the loss of possessions is occasioned by the loss of pleasures.[241]

26.   Trees do not revile nor can they be pleased with effort. When might I dwell with those whose company is a delight?[242]

27.   After dwelling in an empty temple, at the foot of a tree, or in caves, when shall I set forth, unconcerned and not looking back?[243]

---

240. **Tibetan:** "Thus, the wise do not become attached, for fear arises from attachment. These [objects of attachment] pass away by themselves, so be firm and know this."

241. This verse is not included in the Tibetan Derge edition.

242. **Tibetan:** "In the forest the deer, birds, and trees do not speak unpleasantly. When shall I dwell with them, whose company brings delight?"

243. **Tibetan:** "When shall I dwell in a cave, an empty temple, or at the foot of a tree, without looking back, and without attachment?"

28. When shall I dwell in unclaimed and naturally spacious regions, wandering as I please and without a residence?[244]

29. When shall I dwell fearlessly, without protecting my body, having a clay bowl as my only property and a garment useless to a thief?[245]

30. When shall I go to the local charnel grounds and compare my own body, which has the nature of decay, with other corpses?

31. For this body of mine will also become so putrid that even the jackals will not come near it because of its stench.

32. If the co-emergent pieces of bones of this single body will fall apart, how much more so another person whom one holds dear?[246]

33. A person is born alone and also dies alone. No one else has a share in one's agony. What is the use of loved ones who create hindrances?

34. Just as one who has undertaken a journey takes lodging, so does one who travels in the cycle of existence take lodging in a rebirth.

35. Until one is hoisted by four men and mourned by the world, one should retire to the forest.

36. Free of intimacy and free of conflict, one is in bodily solitude. One has already died to the world and does not grieve when dying.[247]

---

244. **Tibetan:** "When shall I dwell, living freely and without attachment, in unclaimed and naturally spacious regions?"

245. **Tibetan:** "When shall I dwell with a paltry alms bowl and so on and clothing wanted by no one, living fearlessly even without concealing my body?"

246. **Tibetan:** "If the flesh and bone that have arisen together with this body will deteriorate and disperse, how much more is this the case for other friends?"

247. **Tibetan:** "Without intimacy and without conflict, one dwells in physical solitude, and when one is counted as if already dead, no one grieves when one actually dies."

37.   No one brings one distress, attending one and grieving, nor are there any who distract one from the recollection of the Buddha and the like.[248]

38.   Therefore, I should always cultivate solitude, which is delightful, without difficulties, having a favorable outcome, and subduing all distractions.[249]

39.   Free from all other concerns and having a single-pointed mind, I shall apply myself to meditative concentration and to the subjugation of the mind.

40.   For sensuous desires create calamities in this world and the next: through imprisonment, beating, and dismemberment in this world, and in hell and the like in the next.[250]

41.   She for whom you have supplicated male and female messengers many times and for whose sake you have not considered the cost of either vice nor disgrace,

42.   Throwing yourself into danger and wasting your wealth, embracing her with the greatest pleasure—

43.   She is nothing but bones, indifferent and impersonal. Why do you not resort to emancipation, fully embracing it to your heart's content?[251]

---

248. **Tibetan:** "There is no one to inflict grief or harm, nor is there anyone to distract one from the recollection of the Buddha and so forth."

249. **Tibetan:** "Thus, I shall always dwell alone in the delightful forest, which creates few problems, good cheer, and the pacification of all distractions."

250. **Tibetan:** "Casting off all other concerns, and with a single-pointed mind, I shall strive to balance and subdue my mind. In this world and the next, sensuous desires create troubles, such as murder, imprisonment, and dismemberment in this life, and hell and so forth in the next."

251. **Tibetan:** "For her sake, male and female messengers first make many supplications, and with no regard for vices or disgrace, I immerse myself in fear and exhaust my wealth. That which gives the greatest pleasure when embraced is nothing but bones; it is neither autonomous nor personal; and yet I lust and crave for it. Then why do I not resort to emancipation?"

44.   Either you have seen that bashfully lowered face before as be-
      ing lifted up with effort, or you have not seen it as it was cov-
      ered by a veil.[252]

45.   Now, that face is revealed by vultures as if they are unable to
      bear your anxiousness. Look at it! Why are you fleeing away
      now?[253]

46.   Jealous one, why do you not protect what was guarded from
      the glances of others, as it is being eaten now?[254]

47.   Seeing this mass of flesh being eaten by vultures and others,
      should you worship others' food with wreaths of flowers, san-
      dalwood paste, and ornaments?

48.   You fear a skeleton that has been seen like this, even though it
      does not move. Why do you not fear it when it moves as if set in
      motion by some ghost?[255]

49.   Their saliva and excrement arise from the same food. Why then
      do you dislike excrement and like sucking saliva?

50.   The enamored, deluded with regard to filth, do not delight in
      pillows stuffed with cotton and soft to the touch because they
      do not emit a foul odor.[256]

51.   You had this passion for it even when it was covered, so why do
      you dislike it when it is uncovered? If you have no use for it,
      why do you caress it when covered?[257]

---

252. **Tibetan:** "First her face is raised with effort, but once raised, it looks down with
modesty. Whether it was previously seen or not, her face is covered by a veil."

253. **Tibetan:** "Just as that face that torments you is perceived now, so will you see it
unveiled by vultures. Why does it make you flee now?"

254. **Tibetan:** "Since you guarded her face from the gaze of others, why do you, O
avaricious one, not guard it as it is being eaten?"

255. In the Tibetan version this verse is followed by the following verse: "You lust
after this even when it is clothed, so why do you not lust after it when it is unclothed
[in the charnel grounds]? If that is pointless, why do you embrace it when clothed?"

256. **Tibetan:** "Taking no delight in cotton pillows that are soft to the touch, the lustful, who are deluded with respect to filth, say [the body] does not emit a foul odor."

257. **Tibetan:** "The lustful, degraded, and deluded have disdain for soft cotton, say-
ing, 'It can't engage in intercourse.'"

52.   If you have no passion for the impure, why do you embrace someone else, who is a skeleton of bones tied by sinews and smeared with a mire of flesh?[258]

53.   You have plenty of filth yourself. Be satisfied with that alone. Voracious for feces! Forget another sack of muck![259]

54.   You desire to look at it and touch it because you like its flesh. How can you desire flesh, which by nature is devoid of consciousness?[260]

55.   The mind that you desire cannot be seen or touched; and that which can be is not conscious. Why do you embrace it in vain?

56.   It is not surprising that you do not look upon another person's body as composed of filth, but it is astonishing that you do not perceive your own body as comprised of filth.

57.   Apart from the delicate, muck-arisen lotus, opening under the rays of the cloudless sun, what delight is there in the cage of filth for a mind addicted to filth?[261]

58.   If you do not desire to touch soil and the like because it is smeared with excrement, how can you desire to touch the body out of which it is excreted?

59.   If you do not have passion for what is impure, why do you embrace someone else, who is a seed arisen from a field of filth and nourished by it?

60.   You do not desire a dirty worm originating from filth because it is small, but you desire a body that consists of much filth and is also born from filth.

---

258. **Tibetan:** "If you say, 'I do not lust after filth,' why do you embrace on your lap something else that is a skeleton tied together with sinews and plastered over with a mire of flesh?"

259. **Tibetan:** "You have plenty of filth yourself, and you always have the use of it, yet out of craving you desire the filth in another sack of muck."

260. **Tibetan:** "Casting aside a fresh lotus opening under the rays of the cloudless sun, why do you, with your filth-craving mind, take delight in a container of muck?"

261. **Tibetan:** "Thinking, 'I like its flesh,' you wish to touch it and look at it. Why do you not desire the flesh [of a dead body], which, by nature, is not sentient?" Note the inversion of vv 54 and 57.

61. Not only do you not abhor your own filthiness, you, voracious for excrement, long for other vessels of filth![262]

62. Even the ground is considered impure when savory foods, such as camphor or boiled rice and condiments, are spat out or vomited from the mouth.

63. If you do not trust that this is filth even though it is obvious, look at other bodies too, repugnant and discarded in the charnel grounds.

64. Knowing that great fear arises when the skin is torn off, how can you have attraction to that same thing again?

65. Although applied to the body, this fragrance is from sandalwood and not from anything else. Why are you attracted to someone by the fragrance that belongs to something else?

66. If attraction does not arise due to a naturally foul smell, is that not good? Why do people take pleasure in what is worthless and anoint it with fragrance?

67. If it is sandalwood that is sweet-smelling, did it come from the body? Why is one attracted to someone because of a fragrance that belongs to something else?

68. If the naked body, containing the slime of filth, is frightening in its natural condition with its long hair and nails and stained yellowish teeth,

69. Why do you meticulously polish it like a weapon for suicide? The earth is crowded with insane people, diligent in deluding themselves.[263]

---

262. **Tibetan:** "Not only do you not abhor your own filth, out of craving you desire other filthy sacks of excrement."

263. **Tibetan:** "If the nature of the body, with its long hair and nails and smelly, yellowish teeth, and befouled with the stench of slime, is frightening in its nakedness, why do I meticulously rub it, like a weapon for my own destruction? This earth is thrown in turmoil by idiots, with their attempts to delude themselves."

70. Seeing a few corpses in a charnel ground, you are repelled, yet you delight in a village which is a charnel ground crowded with moving corpses.[264]

71. Also, although this body is filth, it is not acquired without a price. For its sake there is exhaustion in earning it and there is agony in hells and the like.[265]

72. A child is not able to earn money. When one is a youth, with what is one happy? The prime of one's life passes away in making a living. What can an old person do with sensual gratification?[266]

73. Some debased sensualists, exhausted by a full day's work, come home in the evening and sleep like the dead.[267]

74. Others are afflicted by the troubles of traveling abroad because of military expeditions. Although longing for their sons and wives, they do not see them for years on end.[268]

75. Deluded by sensual desires, they sell themselves for that which they never acquire. Instead, their life is uselessly spent in labor for others.

76. The wives of those who have sold themselves and who always carry out commissions give birth at the feet of trees in the jungles and other inopportune places.

---

264. **Tibetan:** "If you are repelled upon seeing just skeletons in a charnel ground, are you attracted to a village which is a charnel ground crowded with animated skeletons?"

265. **Tibetan:** "Thus, that filth is not gained without a price. Due to accomplishing that end, one is afflicted with fatigue and torments in hells."

266. **Tibetan:** "A child cannot increase its wealth, so with what is one happy when one is a youth? When one's life is spent accumulating wealth, what good is sensual gratification once one is old?"

267. **Tibetan:** "Some debased sensualists exhaust themselves with work throughout the day; then upon coming home, their depleted bodies fall asleep like the dead."

268. **Tibetan:** "Others are afflicted by traveling abroad and suffer as they are far from home; and though they long for their wives and children, they do not see them for years on end."

77. In order to make a livelihood, they enter war that endangers their lives, and they become servants for the sake of their self-respect. They are fools ridiculed for their sensual desires.

78. Some other sensualists are mutilated, fixed on a stake. They are seen being burned and slain with daggers.

79. Consider wealth as an unending misfortune because of the troubles of acquiring, protecting, and losing it. Those whose minds are attached to wealth on account of their distracted state have no opportunity for liberation from the suffering of mundane existence.[269]

80. Thus, sensualists have much distress and little enjoyment, like a beast that has hold of a bit of grass while pulling a wagon.

81. For the sake of that bit of enjoyment, which is easily attainable even for an animal, an ill-fated one has destroyed this leisure and endowment, which is very difficult to find.

82. This exertion is constantly made for the sake of the body, which is definitely transient, insignificant, and falls into hells and the like.[270]

83. With even a billionth part of that diligence, there can be Buddhahood. Sensualists have suffering greater than the suffering of the Path, but they have no Awakening.

84. After bringing to mind the anguish of hell and the like, neither a weapon, poison, fire, a precipice, nor enemies are comparable to sensual desires.[271]

85. Fearing sensual desires in this way, one should generate delight in solitude and in deserted woodlands devoid of strife and annoyances.[272]

---

269. **Tibetan:** "...Those who are distracted by attachment to wealth have no opportunity for liberation from the suffering of mundane existence."

270. **Tibetan:** "Sensual gratification is definitely transient and it casts one down to hell and so forth, and for no great end one is constantly wearied."

271. **Tibetan:** "If one considers the suffering of the hells and so on, weapons, poison, fire, precipices, and enemies do not compare to sensual desires."

272. **Tibetan:** "Becoming disillusioned with sensual desires in that way, generate delight in solitude in the peaceful forest, devoid of strife and annoyances."

86.   The fortunate ones, caressed by silent and gentle forest breezes, pace on pleasant boulders, spacious like palaces, cooled by sandalwood-like moon rays, and ponder how to benefit others.[273]

87.   Dwelling here and there for as long as one likes, freed from the exhaustion of guarding one's possessions and free of care, one lives as one pleases in an empty dwelling, at the foot of a tree, or in a cave.[274]

88.   Living as one wishes, homeless, and not tied down by anyone, one savors the joy of contentment, which is difficult even for a king to find.[275]

89.   After meditating on the advantages of solitude in this and other ways, having one's discursive thoughts calmed, one should cultivate the Spirit of Awakening.[276]

90.   One should first earnestly meditate on the equality of oneself and others in this way: "All equally experience suffering and happiness, and I must protect them as I do myself."[277]

91.   Just as the body, which has many parts owing to its division into arms and so forth, should be protected as a whole, so should this entire world, which is differentiated and yet has the nature of the same suffering and happiness.[278]

---

273. **Tibetan:** "The fortunate, pondering how to benefit others, roam about, caressed by silent, gentle forest breezes and cooled by the sandalwood rays of the moon on the lovely mansions of vast boulders."

274. **Tibetan:** "In an empty hut, at the foot of a tree, or in a cave, one remains as long as one desires; and casting off the suffering of guarding one's possessions, one lives lightheartedly, without a care."

275. **Tibetan:** "Living freely, without attachment, and not tied by anyone, one savors the joy of contentment that is difficult even for a king to find."

276. **Tibetan:** "After considering the advantages of solitude in such ways, one should calm ideation and cultivate the Spirit of Awakening."

277. **Tibetan:** "...Since all are alike in terms of joy and sorrow, I should protect everyone as I do myself."

278. **Tibetan:** "Although it has many divisions, such as its arms and so on, the body is protected as a whole. Likewise, different beings, with their joys and sorrows, are all equal, like myself, in their yearning for happiness."

92. Although my suffering does not cause pain in other bodies, nevertheless that suffering is mine and is difficult to bear because of my attachment to myself.[279]

93. Likewise, although I myself do not feel the suffering of another person, that suffering belongs to that person and is difficult [for him] to bear because of his attachment to himself.[280]

94. I should eliminate the suffering of others because it is suffering, just like my own suffering. I should take care of others because they are sentient beings, just as I am a sentient being.

95. When happiness is equally dear to others and myself, then what is so special about me that I strive after happiness for myself alone?

96. When fear and suffering are equally abhorrent to others and myself, then what is so special about me that I protect myself but not others?

97. If I do not protect them because I am not afflicted by their suffering, why do I protect my body from the suffering of a future body, which is not my pain?[281]

98. The assumption that "it is the same me even then" is false; because it is one person who has died and quite another who is born.[282]

99. If one thinks that the suffering that belongs to someone is to be warded off by that person himself, then why does the hand protect the foot when the pain of the foot does not belong to the hand?[283]

---

279. **Tibetan:** "Even though my agony does not hurt anyone else's body, that suffering of mine is unbearable because I cling to it as mine."

280. **Tibetan:** "Likewise, although others' suffering does not descend upon me, that suffering of theirs is difficult to bear because they cling to it as theirs."

281. **Tibetan:** "...then why do I guard against future suffering when it does not harm me [now]?"

282. **Tibetan:** "The notion that I will experience that is mistaken, for the one who has died is born elsewhere and is someone else."

283. **Tibetan:** "If one thinks a person's suffering should be warded off by himself, since pain of the foot is not of the hand, why should the one take care of the other?"

100. If one argues that even though it is inappropriate, it happens because of grasping onto a self, our response is: With all one's might, one should avoid that which is inappropriate, whether it belongs to oneself or to another.

101. The continuum of consciousness, like a series, and the aggregation of constituents, like an army and such, are unreal.[284] Since one who experiences suffering does not exist, to whom will that suffering belong?

102. All sufferings are without an owner, because they are not different. They should be warded off simply because they are suffering. Why is any restriction made in this case?[285]

103. Why should suffering be prevented? Because everyone agrees. If it must be warded off, then all of it must be warded off; and if not, then this goes for oneself as it does for everyone else.[286]

104. [Qualm:] Much suffering comes from compassion, so why should one force it to arise?
[Response:] After seeing the suffering of the world, how can this suffering from compassion be considered great?

---

284. The *Pañjikā*, pp. 158-159, reads: "A continuum *(saṃtāna)* does not exist as some ultimately existent unity. However, it has the form of a successive stream of moments that have arisen as the condition of causes and effects, because of the nonperceptibility of a distinct [moment]. Therefore, for the sake of convention, the Buddhas have used the term *continuum* as a nominal designation in order to explain those moments with one word. Hence, it exists only as a designation. Therefore, one should not insist on that. Likewise, because of the non-recognition of a single [member] from those other members, an aggregation does not exist as a single thing consisting of combining elements. It does not follow from this that a false notion with regard to reality as being different has disappeared as a result of the investigation of the members of this [aggregation]. Thus, this [aggregation], too, is only conventionally existent."

285. **Tibetan:** "As there is no owner of miseries, there are no distinctions among them all. They are to be dispelled because they are suffering. What is the use of restrictions there?"

286. **Tibetan:** [Qualm:] "Why should everyone's suffering be counteracted?"
[Response:] "There is no argument: If it is to be averted, everyone's is to be averted. If not, [remember] I am like [other] sentient beings."

105. If the suffering of many disappears because of the suffering of one, then a compassionate person should induce that suffering for his own sake and for the sake of others.

106. Therefore, Supuṣpacandra, although knowing the king's animosity, did not avoid his own suffering as a sacrifice for many people in misery.[287]

107. Thus, those whose mind-streams are cultivated in meditation and who equally accept the suffering of others dive into the Avīci hell like swans into a pool of lotuses.[288]

108. They become oceans of joy when sentient beings are liberated. Have they not found fulfillment? What is the use of sterile liberation?[289]

109. Thus, although working for the benefit of others, there is neither conceit nor dismay; and on account of the thirst for the single goal of benefiting others, there is no desire for the result of the maturation of one's *karma*.[290]

110. Therefore, to the extent that I protect myself from disparagement, so shall I generate a spirit of protection and a spirit of compassion toward others.[291]

111. Due to habituation, there is a sense that "I" exists in the drops of blood and semen that belong to others, even though the being in question does not exist.

---

287. The story of the Bodhisattva Supuṣpacandra appears in the *Samādhirājasūtra*, Buddhist Sanskrit Texts Series, no. 2, pp. 160-161.

288. **Tibetan:** "Thus, one whose mind-stream is accustomed to meditation and who delights in calming the suffering of others enters into Avīci hell like a swan into a pool of lotuses."

289. **Tibetan:** "When sentient beings are liberated, they have oceans of joy. Is that not enough? What is the point of desiring one's own liberation?"

290. **Tibetan:** "Thus, even though one serves the needs of others, one has no conceit or amazement. Due to delighting solely in others' welfare, one has no hope for the result of the maturation of one's *karma*."

291. **Tibetan:** "Therefore, just as I protect myself from even minor disparagement, so shall I generate a spirit of protection and a spirit of compassion toward others."

112. Why do I not also consider another's body as myself in the same way, since the otherness of my own body is not difficult to determine?

113. Acknowledging oneself as fault-ridden and others as oceans of virtues, one should contemplate renouncing one's self-identity and accepting others.[292]

114. Just as the hands and the like are cherished because they are members of the body, why are embodied beings not cherished in the same way, for they are the members of the world?

115. Just as the notion of a self with regard to one's own body, which has no personal existence, is due to habituation, will the identity of one's self with others not arise out of habituation in the same way?

116. Although working for the benefit of others in this way, there is neither conceit nor dismay. Even upon feeding oneself, expectation of a reward does not arise.

117. Therefore, just as you wish to protect yourself from pain, grief, and the like, so may you cultivate a spirit of protection and a spirit of compassion toward the world.[293]

118. Therefore the protector Avalokita empowered his own name to remove even one's fear arising from timidity in front of an audience.[294]

119. One should not turn away from difficulty, since owing to the power of habituation, one may have no pleasure in the absence of something that one previously feared to hear mentioned.

120. One who wishes to protect oneself and others quickly should practice exchanging oneself for others, which is a great mystery.

---

292. **Tibetan:** "Having recognized oneself as faulty and others as oceans of virtues, one should practice discarding self-grasping and accepting others."

293. **Tibetan:** "Therefore, just as you protect yourself from even minor disparagement, cultivate a spirit of protection and a spirit of compassion toward the world."

294. **Tibetan:** "Hence, out of great compassion Lord Avalokita blessed his own name to dispel even the anxiety of being in a crowd."

121. If even at a small danger fear arises on account of great attachment to oneself, why would one not abhor that self like a terrifying enemy?

122. One who kills birds, fish, and deer and sets up an ambush with the desire to quell illness, thirst, and hunger,

123. One who kills one's parents and steals the property of the Three Jewels for the sake of profit and respect, will become fuel in the Avici hell.[295]

124. What wise person would desire, protect, and venerate such a self? Who would not see it as an enemy and who would respect it?

125. If out of concern for oneself one thinks: "If I give it away, what shall I enjoy?" this is a fiendish state. If out of concern for others one thinks: "If I enjoy it, what shall I give away?" this is a divine state.[296]

126. Upon harming another for one's own sake, one is burnt in hells and the like; but upon afflicting oneself for the sake of others, one has success in everything.

127. The desire for self-aggrandizement leads to a miserable state of existence, low status, and stupidity. By transferring that same desire to someone else, one obtains a fortunate state of existence, respect, and wisdom.

128. By ordering another around for one's own sake, one experiences the position of a servant and the like; but by ordering oneself around for the sake of others, one experiences the position of a master and the like.

---

295. **Tibetan:** "Out of a desire to quell such pains as hunger and thirst, one kills birds, fish, and deer, and waits in ambush. For the sake of profit and respect, one even kills one's parents and steals the property of the Three Jewels, and thus burns in Avici."

296. **Tibetan:** "'If I give something away, what shall I enjoy?' Concern for one's own welfare is the attitude of a demon. 'If I enjoy something, what shall I give?' Concern for others' welfare is the approach of the gods."

129. All those who are unhappy in the world are so as a result of their desire for their own happiness. All those who are happy in the world are so as a result of their desire for the happiness of others.[297]

130. Enough of much talk! Note the difference between the fool who seeks his own benefit and the sage who works for the benefit of others.

131. One who does not exchange his own happiness for the suffering of others surely does not achieve Buddhahood. How could one find happiness even in the cycle of existence?

132. Not to mention the next life, even in this life, a desired goal of a servant who does not do his work and of a master who does not pay out the wages cannot be accomplished.[298]

133. Forsaking the generation of mutual happiness and the felicity of present and future happiness, deluded people take on tremendous suffering because of harming one another.[299]

134. If the whole range of adversities, sufferings, and fears in the world arises from grasping onto the self, what use is this grasping to me?[300]

135. Without forsaking one's own self, one cannot avoid suffering, just as without avoiding fire one cannot avoid being burned.

136. Therefore, in order to alleviate my own suffering and to alleviate the suffering of others, I give myself up to others and I accept others as my own self.

---

297. **Tibetan:** "All the joy in the world comes from the desire for others' happiness, and all the suffering in the world comes from the desire for one's own happiness."

298. **Tibetan:** "Not to mention the next life, a servant would not do his work, and a master would not pay out wages, so not even the goals of this life are accomplished."

299. **Tibetan:** "Forsaking the bountiful felicity that brings about seen and unseen happiness, due to inflicting suffering on others, deluded people take on unbearable suffering."

300. **Tibetan:** "If all the harm, fear, and suffering in the world occur due to grasping onto the self, what use is that great demon to me?"

137. O mind, make this resolve: "I am bound to others." From now on you must not be concerned with anything but the welfare of all sentient beings.

138. It is inappropriate to seek one's own welfare with the eyes and so on that are dedicated to others. It is inappropriate to pour one's own benefit with hands that are dedicated to others.[301]

139. Therefore, becoming subservient to sentient beings and snatching away whatever you see on this body, use it for the well-being of others.[302]

140. Placing your own identity in inferior ones and placing the identity of others in your own self, cultivate envy and pride with the mind free of discursive thoughts.[303]

141. He is respected, not I. I am not wealthy as he is. He is praised, while I am despised. I am unhappy, while he is happy.

142. I do chores while he lives at ease. It seems he is great in the world, while I am debased, lacking good qualities.[304]

143. What can one do without good qualities? Every person is endowed with good qualities. There are those with regard to whom I am inferior, and there are those with regard to whom I am superior.

144. Due to the power of mental afflictions, the degeneration of my views and ethical discipline is not under my control. I must be cured as far as possible. I even accept the pain.[305]

---

301. **Tibetan:** "It is wrong to accomplish my own welfare with eyes and so forth that are subservient to others, and it is wrong for the eyes and so forth to treat them improperly."

302. **Tibetan:** "Therefore, regarding others as most important, snatch away whatever you see on your body and use it to benefit them."

303. **Tibetan:** "Identifying yourself as inferior and so forth, and identifying others as yourself, with the mind free of ideation, cultivate jealousy, competitiveness, and pride."

304. **Tibetan:** "I do all the work while this one lives at ease, and it is well known that this one is great in the world, while I am debased and lacking good qualities."

305. **Tibetan:** "The degeneration of my ethical discipline, views, and so on is due to the power of mental afflictions and not my own free will. You must heal me as well as you can, and I shall accept the pain."

145. If he cannot cure me, why does he disdain me? What use are his good qualities to me when he is one who has good qualities?

146. He has no compassion for beings who dwell in the jaws of the beast of prey of miserable states of existence. Moreover, out of pride in his qualities, he desires to surpass the wise.

147. Seeing himself as being equal to others, in order to enhance his own superiority, he will obtain wealth and respect for himself even by means of discord.

148. Were my good qualities to become apparent to everyone in the world, then no one would even hear of his good qualities.[306]

149. Were my faults to be concealed, there would be honor for me and not for him. Today, I have easily acquired possessions. I am honored while he is not.

150. Delighted, we shall watch him as he is finally being ill-treated, ridiculed, and reviled from all sides.

151. Also, it seems this wretched one is competing with me. Does he have this much learning, wisdom, beauty, noble ancestry, and wealth?[307]

152. Hearing my own good qualities being praised everywhere in this way, thrilled, with my hair standing on end, I shall enjoy the delight of happiness.[308]

153. Even though he has wealth, we should forcibly seize it from him and give him mere sustenance if he works for us.[309]

---

306. **Tibetan:** "Regarding those who are equal to myself, in order to establish my own superiority, my wealth and honor are to be gained even with discord. In any case, may my good qualities become obvious to the whole world, and may no one hear of the good qualities of this one."

307. **Tibetan:** "It has come out that this miserable being is competing with me. Are his learning, wisdom, beauty, lineage, and wealth equal to mine?"

308. **Tibetan:** "Thus, hearing my own good qualities proclaimed to everyone, I experience a joy that makes my hair stand on end with delight."

309. **Tibetan:** "Even though this one has possessions, they are to be taken over with my strength; and if he works for me, I will give him just enough to survive."

154. We should deprive him of happiness and always yoke him to our anguish. We all have been afflicted in the cycle of existence hundreds of times by him.

155. Countless eons have passed away while you sought your own benefit. With this great toil you have gained only suffering.[310]

156. At my request, apply yourself in this way right now without hesitation. Later you will see the advantages of this, for the words of the Sage are true.[311]

157. If you had carried out this task earlier, this state deprived of the perfection and bliss of the Buddha would not have occurred.[312]

158. Therefore, just as you formed a sense of self-identity with regard to the drops of blood and semen of others, contemplate others in the same way.[313]

159. Living as one who belongs to others and snatching away whatever you see on this body, practice what is beneficial for others.[314]

160. Arouse envy toward your own self in this way: I am well while the other is miserable; the other is lowly while I am exalted; the other works while I do not.[315]

---

310. **Tibetan:** "O mind, countless eons have passed as you have yearned to accomplish your own self-interest, but with such great toil you have gained only suffering."

311. **Tibetan:** "Thus, definitely apply yourself to the interests of others; and you will see the advantages of that, for the words of the Sage are infallible."

312. **Tibetan:** "If you had done this earlier, a situation such as this, which is not the excellence and bliss of a Buddha, would never have occurred."

313. **Tibetan:** "Therefore, just as you have identified with the I in the drops of blood and semen of others, so accustom yourself to others."

314. **Tibetan:** "Having become a scout for others, snatch away whatever appears on your body, and live to benefit others."

315. **Tibetan:** "Why do you not arouse envy, thinking, 'I am happy, while others are not; I am high, while others are low; and I do what is beneficial, while others do not'?"

161. Deprive yourself of happiness and expose yourself to the suffering of others. Examine your pretense in this way: "What do I do at what time?"[316]

162. Take the mistake made by another on your head, and disclose even a trivial mistake of yours to the Great Sage.[317]

163. Cover up your own fame with accounts of surpassing glory of others, and drive yourself, like a despised slave, into works for sentient beings.[318]

164. This one should not be praised for a trace of an adventitious good quality, for he is full of faults. Act so that no one may know of your good qualities.[319]

165. In brief, whatever offense you have committed toward others for your own benefit, let it descend on yourself for the benefit of sentient beings.[320]

166. This one should not be encouraged to be abusive, but should be established in the behavior of a young bride, modest, meek, and restrained.[321]

167. Act in this way! Remain in this way! You should not do this! You should be subjugated and subdued in this way if you disobey.[322]

---

316. **Tibetan:** "Deprive yourself of happiness, and take on the suffering of others. Examine your own faults with the consideration, 'What have I done at what time?'"

317. **Tibetan:** "Take the blame yourself for others' mistakes, and if you commit even a small misdeed, confess it to many people."

318. **Tibetan:** "Let your own reputation be outshone by exalting the reputation of others, and like the least of servants, commit yourself to everyone's welfare."

319. **Tibetan:** "This one of defective nature should not be praised for adventitious good qualities. Act so that no one may know of this one's good qualities."

320. **Tibetan:** "In brief, let whatever harm you have inflicted on others for your own benefit descend on you for the sake of sentient beings."

321. **Tibetan:** "This one should not be encouraged to be aggressive, but induced to be shy, meek, and restrained, in the manner of a young bride."

322. **Tibetan:** "Do that and remain in that way. [If] you do not act like that, you are to be subjugated; and if you transgress that [discipline], you are to be subdued."

168. O mind, if you do not do this even when you are being told, then I shall subjugate you alone, for all faults dwell in you.

169. Where will you go? I can see you, and I shall annihilate all your vanities. That was another, earlier time when I was ruined by you.

170. Now give up this hope: "Still, I have my own self-interest"! Unconcerned as you are with much distress, I have sold you to others.³²³

171. If I do not joyfully offer you to sentient beings, you will undoubtedly deliver me to the guardians of hell.

172. Handing me over in that way many times, you have tormented me for a long time. Remembering those grudges, I shall destroy you, the servant of your own self-interest.³²⁴

173. If you are pleased with yourself, you should take no pleasure in yourself. If you need protection, it is inappropriate to protect yourself.³²⁵

174. The more this body is pampered, the more fragile it becomes and the more it degenerates.³²⁶

175. When it has degenerated in this way, not even this earth can completely fulfill its desire. Who will then satisfy its desire?

176. For one who desires the impossible, mental affliction and disappointment arise; but for one who is free of expectations, there is unblemished prosperity.

---

323. **Tibetan:** "Now cast off the thought, 'I still have my own self-interest'! I have sold you to others, so offer your strength without dismay!"

324. **Tibetan:** "By handing me over in that way, you have long tormented me. Now, remembering those grudges, I shall destroy your self-centered attitude."

325. **Tibetan:** "If you wish for your own pleasure, you should not take pleasure in yourself. If you wish to protect yourself, you should always protect others."

326. **Tibetan:** "The more the body is pampered, the more exceedingly fragile it becomes."

177. Therefore, free rein should not be given to the growth of bodily desires. It is truly good when one does not take something that one wants.[327]

178. This awful, impure form has its end in ashes and stillness, moved only by another. Why do I grasp onto it as mine?

179. Of what use is this contrivance to me, whether it is dead or alive? What difference is there between this and a clump of soil and the like? Alas, you are not eliminating the grasping onto the "I"![328]

180. By favoring the body, one uselessly accumulates suffering. Of what use is anger or love to something equal to a piece of wood?

181. Whether it is nurtured by me or eaten by vultures, it feels neither affection nor aversion, so why am I fond of it?

182. If the body, which has no anger due to abuse nor satisfaction due to praise, is unconscious, then for whom am I exerting myself?

183. Those who like this body are said to be my friends. They all like their own bodies, too, so why do I not like them?

184. Therefore, with indifference I have given up my body for the benefit of the world. Hence, although it has many faults, I keep it as an instrument for that task.

---

327. **Tibetan:** "Therefore, since bodily desires increase, they should not be given free rein. Something attractive which is not grasped is a good thing."

328. **Tibetan:** "Of what use is this machine to me, dead or alive? What difference is there between this and a clump of soil and so forth? Alas, that you do not dispel pride!"

185. So enough of worldly conduct! Recalling the teaching on conscientiousness and warding off drowsiness and lethargy, I shall
follow the wise.[329]

186. Therefore, withdrawing the mind from evil ways, I shall always
concentrate it on its own meditative object to eliminate
obscurations.[330]

---

329. **Tibetan:** "Thus, enough of foolish behavior! I shall follow the wise; and, bearing in mind the advice on conscientiousness, I shall ward off drowsiness and
lethargy."

The following verse appears in the Tibetan version, but not in the Sanskrit: "Like
the compassionate Children of the Jinas, I shall endure the rigors of righteousness. If
I do not constantly strive day and night, when will my suffering ever come to an
end?"

330. **Tibetan:** "Therefore, in order to eliminate obscurations, I shall withdraw the
mind from evil ways and shall always concentrate on a true meditative object."

Chapter IX
The Perfection of Wisdom

1. The Sage taught this entire system for the sake of wisdom. There-
    fore, with the desire to ward off suffering, one should develop
    wisdom.

2. This truth is recognized as being of two kinds: conventional and
    ultimate.[331] Ultimate reality is beyond the scope of the intellect.
    The intellect is called conventional reality.[332]

---

331. The *Pañjikā*, pp. 170-171, defines conventional and ultimate realities in this way:
"Conventional reality is that which conceals and obscures the complete knowledge
of things as they are *(yathā-bhūta)* because it obscures with [the belief in] an intrinsic
nature *(svabhāva)* and explains with that which is obscured. Its synonyms are ignorance *(avidyā)*, delusion *(moha)*, and misunderstanding *(viparyāsa)*." The *Pañjikā* also
states that conventional truth is of two kinds: true conventional truth *(tathyasaṃvṛti)*
and false conventional truth *(mithyāsaṃvṛti)*. "An appearance of an object, such as
the color blue, etc., that has originated in dependence on something else and is perceived by accurate sense-faculties is usually true; however, [the appearance of an
object] that has originated in dependence on an illusion, mirage, or reflection, that is
perceived by faulty sense-faculties, or is fabricated by the scriptures of heterodox
groups *(tīrthika)* is usually false....Both [conventional truths] are false for the Āryas,
who see correctly, because in the state of ultimate truth, conventional truth is false.
Ultimate truth *(paramārtha)* is the highest, ultimate reality, the true *(akṛtrima)* nature
of phenomena. On account of understanding [the true nature of phenomena], mental afflictions *(kleśa)*, the series of karmic imprints *(vāsanā)*, and all obscurations
(āvaraṇa) are eliminated. Its synonyms are the lack of the intrinsic nature
(niḥsvabhāvatā) of all phenomena, emptiness *(śūnyatā)*, thusness *(tathatā)*, the pin-
nacle of existence *(bhūta-koṭi)*, and the sphere of reality *(dharma-dhātu)*, etc."

332. The *Pañjikā*, p. 177, reads: "Intellect is called conventional reality because every
intellect has the nature of conceptualization *(vikalpa)* regarding an object *(ālambana)*
that is no object *(nirālambana)*; and every conceptualization is of the nature of spiritual ignorance *(avidyā)* because it apprehends unreality. As [a Mādhyamika] states:
'This conceptualization itself has acquired the nature of spiritual ignorance,' and
spiritual ignorance is conventional truth. It is proper to say that no intellect ultimately apprehends the nature of ultimate truth."

3.   In the light of this, people are seen to be of two types: the con-templative[333] and the ordinary person. The ordinary folks are superseded by the contemplatives.[334]

4.   Due to the difference in their intelligence, even contemplatives are refuted by successively higher ones by means of analogies accepted by both parties,[335] regardless of what they aim to prove.

5.   Ordinary people see and imagine things as real and not illusory. It is in this respect that there is disagreement between the contemplatives and the ordinary people.

6.   Even the objects of direct perception, such as form and the like, are established by consensus and not by verifying cognition. That consensus is false, as is the general agreement that pure things are impure, for example.

7.   The Protector taught things[336] in order to bring people to understanding.
[Qualm:] If these things are not ultimately, but only conventionally, momentary, this is inconsistent.

8.   [Mādhyamika:] There is no fault in the conventional truth of the contemplatives. In contrast to ordinary people, they see reality. Otherwise, ordinary people would invalidate the perception of women as impure.

---

333. According to the Pañjikā, p. 178, a contemplative is one who has yoga, that is, meditative concentration (samādhi) that is characterized by non-perception of all phenomena.

334. According to the Pañjikā, p. 178, an ordinary person (prākṛta) is one born of the nature (prakṛti) that is spiritual ignorance (avidyā) and craving (tṛṣṇā), the cause of the origination of the cycle of existence (saṃsāra). A contemplative perceives undistorted essential reality, and an ordinary person perceives the distorted reality of phenomena on account of being mistaken. An ordinary person's opinion is determined to be false by a contemplative.

335. According to the Pañjikā, p. 179, "analogies (dṛṣṭānta) such as an illusion, mirage, the reflection of a city of gandharvas, and so on, which are mentioned by the Blessed One in the sūtras, are established by both [contemplatives and ordinary people] as lacking intrinsic nature."

336. According to the Pañjikā, p. 181, "the aggregates (skandha), sense-bases (āyatana), etc."

9. *[Qualm:]* How can there possibly be merit due to the Jina who is like an illusion, as is the case if he is truly existent? If a sentient being is like an illusion, why is he born again after he dies?

10. *[Mādhyamika:]* Even an illusion lasts for as long as the collection of its conditions. Why should a sentient being truly exist merely because its continuum lasts a long time?

11. *[Yogācārin:]* If consciousness does not exist, there is no sin in killing an illusory person.
    [Mādhyamika:] On the contrary, when one is endowed with the illusion of consciousness, vice and merit do arise.

12. *[Yogācārin:]* An illusory mind is not possible, since mantras and the like are unable to produce it.
    [Mādhyamika:] Diverse illusions originate on account of diverse conditions. Nowhere does a single condition have the ability to produce everything.

13. *[Yogācārin:]* If one could be ultimately emancipated and yet transmigrate conventionally, then even the Buddha would transmigrate. So what would be the point of the Bodhisattva way of life?

14. *[Mādhyamika:]* When its conditions are not destroyed, an illusion does not cease either. Due to a discontinuity of its conditions, it does not originate even conventionally.

15. *[Yogācārin:]* When even a mistaken cognition does not exist, by what is an illusion ascertained?

16. *[Mādhyamika:]* If for you an illusion itself does not exist, what is apprehended? Even if it is an aspect of the mind itself, in reality it exists as something different.[337]

---

337. The *Pañjikā*, p. 187, "In reality, it exists as something other than the inner (*āntara*) aspect of the mind, which is the apprehender (*grāhaka*)."

17. *[Yogācārin:]* If the mind itself is an illusion, then what is perceived by what?
     [Mādhyamika:] The Protector of the World stated that the mind does not perceive the mind. Just as a sword cannot cut itself, so it is with the mind.

18. *[Yogācārin:]* It illuminates itself, as does a lamp.
     [Mādhyamika:] A lamp does not illuminate itself, for it is not concealed by darkness.

19. *[Yogācārin:]* A blue object does not require something else for its blueness, as does a crystal. So something may or may not occur in dependence on something else.

20. *[Mādhyamika:]* As in the case of non-blueness, blue is not regarded as its own cause. What blue by itself could make itself blue?[338]

21. *[Yogācārin:]* It is said that a lamp illuminates once this is cognized with awareness. The mind is said to illuminate once this is cognized with what?[339]

22. *[Mādhyamika:]* If no one perceives whether the mind is luminous or not, then there is no point in discussing it, like the beauty of a barren woman's daughter.

23. *[Yogācārin:]* If self-cognizing awareness does not exist, how is consciousness recalled?
     [Mādhyamika:] Recollection comes from its relation to something else that was experienced, like a rat's poison.[340]

---

338. This final line is missing in the Tibetan version.

339. According to Minayef, this is the verse 22. P. L. Vaidya's edition follows Minayef's numbering of verses by omitting the number 21.

340. According to the *sPyod 'jug rnam bshad rgyal sras 'jug ngogs*, p. 222, the analogy here refers to an animal, such as a bear, which while sleeping is bitten and infected by a rat. Although the bear is not conscious of being poisoned at the time it is bitten, it "recalls" this upon waking up and sensing the inflammation of the bite.

24.   *[Yogācārin:]* It illuminates itself, because the mind endowed with other conditions perceives.[341]
      [Mādhyamika:] A jar seen due to the application of a magical ointment is not the ointment itself.

25.   The manner in which something is seen, heard, or cognized is not what is refuted here, but the conceptualization of its true existence, which is the cause of suffering, is rejected here.

26.   If you fancy that an illusion is neither different from the mind nor non-different, then if it is a really existing thing, how can it not be different? If it is not different, then it does not really exist.

27.   Just as an illusion can be seen even though it does not truly exist, so it is with the observer, the mind.
      [Yogācārin:] The cycle of existence has its basis in reality or else it would be like space.

28.   *[Mādhyamika:]* How can something that does not exist have any efficacy by being based on something real? You have approached the mind as being an isolated unity.

29.   If the mind were free of any apprehended object, then all beings would be Tathāgatas. Thus, what good is gained by speculating that only the mind exists?

30.   *[Yogācārin:]* Even when the similarity to illusion is recognized, how does a mental affliction cease, since lust for an illusory woman arises even in the one who created her?

31.   *[Mādhyamika:]* Because her creator's imprints of mental afflictions toward objects of knowledge have not been eliminated, when seeing her, his imprint of emptiness is weak.

32.   By building up the imprints of emptiness, the imprint of existence is diminished; and after accustoming oneself to the fact that nothing truly exists, even that diminishes.

---

341. According to the *Pañjikā*, p. 192, the "other conditions" are the mind endowed with knowledge of the future and with extrasensory perception such as awareness of others' thoughts, etc. The thrust of this argument is that if it is possible, under certain conditions, for the mind to perceive the minds of others, then it should be possible for the mind to perceive itself.

33.   *[Yogācārin:]* If it is conceived that a phenomenon that does not really exist cannot be perceived, then how can a non-entity, which is without basis, stand before the mind?

34.   *[Mādhyamika:]* When neither an entity nor a non-entity remains before the mind, then since there is no other possibility, having no objects, it becomes calm.

35.   Just as a wish-fulfilling gem or a wish-granting tree satisfies desires, so the image of the Jina is seen, because of his vow and his disciples.

36.   When a charmer against poisons dies after completing a pillar,[342] that pillar neutralizes poisons and the like, even a long time after his death.

37.   Likewise, the pillar of the Jina, completed in accordance with the Bodhisattva way of life, accomplishes all tasks, even when the Bodhisattva has passed into *nirvāna*.

38.   *[Hīnayānist:]* How could worship offered to something that has no consciousness be fruitful?
       [Mādhyamika:] Because it is taught that it is the same whether he is present or has passed into *nirvāna*.

39.   According to the scriptures, effects of worship do exist, whether conventionally or ultimately, in the same way that worship offered to the true Buddha is said to be fruitful.

40.   *[Hīnayānist:]* Liberation comes from understanding the [Four Noble] Truths, so what is the point of perceiving emptiness?
       [Mādhyamika:] Because a scripture states that there is no Awakening without this path.

41.   *[Hīnayānist:]* The Mahāyāna is certainly not authenticated.
       [Mādhyamika:] How is your scripture authenticated?
       [Hīnayānist:] Because it is authenticated by both of us.
       [Mādhyamika:] Then it is not authenticated by you from the beginning.

---

342. According to the *Pañjikā*, p. 200, it is a pillar made of wood and consecrated with mantras.

42.   Apply the same faith and respect to the Mahāyāna as you do to it. If something is true because it is accepted by two different parties, then the *Vedas* and the like[343] would also be true.

43.   If you object that the Mahāyāna is controversial, then reject your own scripture because it is contested by heterodox groups and because parts of your scriptures are contested by your own people and others.

44.   The teaching has its root in the monkhood, and the monkhood is not on a firm footing. For those whose minds are subject to grasping, *nirvāṇa* is not on a firm footing either.

45.   If your objection is that liberation is due to the elimination of mental afflictions, then it should occur immediately afterward. Yet one can see the power of karma over those people,[344] even though they had no mental afflictions.

46.   If you think that as long as there is no craving there is no grasping onto rebirth, why could their craving, even though free of mental afflictions, not exist as delusion?[345]

47.   Craving has its cause in feeling, and they have feeling. The mind that has mental objects has to dwell on one thing or another.[346]

---

343. According to the *Pañjikā*, p. 205, the phrase "and the like" implies the teachings of] Kaṇāda, also known also as Kāśyapa, an author of the Vaiśeṣika school of the Nyāya philosophy, who taught that the world was formed by the aggregation of atoms, etc.

344. The *Pañjikā*, p. 208: "In Ārya Maudgalyāyana, Ārya Aṅgulimāla, etc."

345. The *Pañjikā*, p. 208: "As the lack of knowledge (*ajñāna*) that is free of mental afflictions." The point here is that according to the *Abhidharmakośa*, there are two types of delusion: afflictive and non-afflictive. Thus, Śāntideva is suggesting that there may similarly be both afflictive and non-afflictive craving and that Śrāvaka Arhats may be subject to non-afflictive craving.

346. According to the *Pañjikā*, p. 209, "on one thing or another" refers either to the Four Noble Truths, etc., that are the domains of attachment, or to the results of meditation on the Four Noble Truths.

48. Without emptiness, the mind is constrained and arises again,[347] as in non-cognitive meditative equipoise. Therefore, one should meditate on emptiness.

49. If you acknowledge the utterances that correspond to the *sūtra*s as the words of the Buddha, why do you not respect the Mahā-yāna, which for the most part is similar to your *sūtra*s?[348]

50. If the whole is faulty because one part is not acceptable, why not consider the whole as taught by the Jina because one part is similar to the *sūtras*?

51. Who will not accept the teachings not fathomed by leaders such as Mahākāśyapa, just because you have failed to understand them?

52. Remaining in the cycle of existence for the sake of those suffering due to delusion is achieved through freedom from attachment and fear. That is a fruit of emptiness.

53. Thus, no refutation is possible with regard to emptiness, so one should meditate on emptiness without hesitation.

54. Since emptiness is the antidote to the darkness of afflictive and cognitive obscurations, how is it that one desiring omniscience does not promptly meditate on it?

55. Let fear arise toward something that produces suffering. Emptiness pacifies suffering. So why does fear of it arise?

56. If there were something called "I," fear could come from anywhere. If there is no "I," whose fear will there be?

57. Teeth, hair, and nails are not I, nor am I bone, blood, mucus, phlegm, pus, or lymph.

---

347. The *Pañjikā*, p. 209, explains this line in the following way: "Without emptiness, that is, leaving emptiness aside, the mind, or consciousness, that has mental objects is constrained by the noose of the attachment toward its object. Although the mind is inactive for some time due to the power of concentration (*samādhi*), it arises again."

348. Verses 50-52 are not found in P. L. Vaidya's 1960 edition. The *Pañjikā*, p. 210, states that those three verses were interpolated by someone, because they have been added to the wrong context and because their author speaks derogatorily of the leaders such as Mahākāśyapa and others.

58. Bodily oil is not I, nor are sweat, fat, or entrails. The cavity of the entrails is not I, nor is excrement or urine.

59. Flesh is not I, nor are sinews, heat, or wind. Bodily apertures are not I, nor, in any way, are the six consciousnesses.

60. If the awareness of sound were I, then sound would always be apprehended. But without an object of awareness, what does it cognize on account of which it is called awareness?[349]

61. If that which is not cognizant were awareness, a piece of wood would be awareness. Therefore, it is certain there is no awareness in the absence of its object.

62. Why does that which cognizes form not hear it as well? [Sāṃkhya:] Because of the absence of sound, there is no awareness of it.[350]

63. [Mādhyamika:] How can something that is of the nature of the apprehension of sound be the apprehension of form? One person may be considered as a father and as a son, but not in terms of ultimate reality,

64. Since sattva, rajas, and tamas are neither a father nor a son. Moreover, its nature is not seen as related to the apprehension of sound.

65. If it is the same thing taking another guise, like an actor, he too is not permanent. If he has different natures, then this unity of his is unprecedented.

66. If another guise is not the true one, then describe its natural appearance. If it were the nature of awareness, then it would follow that all people would be identical.

---

349. According to the sPyod 'jug rnam bshad rgyal sras 'jug ngogs, p. 242, verses 60-67 present a refutation of the Sāṃkhya view.

350. According to sPyod 'jug rnam bshad rgyal sras 'jug ngogs, p. 243, verse 62 in the first line asks: If there were a permanent Self, as the Sāṃkhyas assert, that cognizes form when sound is absent, why would it not also cognize sound at that time, for it is said to be a permanent entity that is totally disengaged from the five sensory objects?

67. That which has volition and that which has no volition would be identical, because their existence would be the same. If difference were false, then what would be the basis for similarity?

68. That which is not conscious is not "I," because it lacks consciousness, like a cloth and the like.[351] If it were conscious because it has consciousness, then it would follow that when it stops being conscious of anything, it would vanish.

69. If the Self is not subject to change, what is the use of its consciousness? Thus, this implies that space, which lacks consciousness and activity, has a Self.

70. [Objection:] Without the Self, the relationship between an action and its result is not possible, for if the agent of an action has perished, who will have the result?

71. [Mādhyamika:] When both of us have agreed that an action and its result have different bases and that the Self has no influence in this matter, then there is no point in arguing about this.

72. One who has the cause cannot possibly be seen as being endowed with the result. It is pointed out that the existence of the agent and the experiencer of the consequences depends on the unity of their continuum of consciousness.

73. The past or future mind is not "I," since it does not exist. If the present mind were "I," then when it had vanished, the "I" would not exist any more.

74. Just as the trunk of a plantain tree is nothing when cut into pieces, in the same way, the "I" is non-existent when sought analytically.

75. [Qualm:] If no sentient being exists, for whom is there compassion? [Mādhyamika:] For one who is imagined through delusion, which is accepted for the sake of the task.

76. [Qualm:] If there is no sentient being, whose is the task? [Mādhyamika:] True. The effort, too, is due to delusion. Nevertheless, in order to alleviate suffering, delusion with regard to one's task is not averted.

---

351. **Tibetan:** "...like a pot and so forth." According to *sPyod 'jug rnam bshad rgyal sras 'jug ngogs*, p. 242, verses 68-69 present a refutation of the Vaiśesika view.

77.   However, grasping onto the "I," which is a cause of suffering, increases because of the delusion with regard to the Self. If this is the unavoidable result of that, meditation on identitylessness is the best.

78.   The body is not the feet, the calves, nor the thighs. Nor is the body the hips, the abdomen, the back, the chest, or the arms.

79.   It is not the hands, the sides of the torso, or the armpits, nor is it characterized by the shoulders. Nor is the body the neck or the head. Then what here is the body?

80.   If this body partially exists in all of these and its parts exist in their parts, where does it stand by itself?

81.   If the body were located in its entirety in the hands and other limbs, there would be just as many bodies as there are hands and so forth.

82.   The body is neither inside nor outside. How can the body be in the hands and other limbs? It is not separate from the hands and the like. How, then, can it be found at all?

83.   Thus, the body does not exist. However, on account of delusion, there is the impression of the body with regard to the hands and the like, because of their specific configuration, just as there is the impression of a person with regard to a pillar.[352]

84.   As long as a collection of conditions lasts, the body appears like a person. Likewise, as long as it lasts with regard to the hands and the like, the body continues to be seen in them.

85.   In the same way, since it is an assemblage of toes, which one would be a foot?[353] The same applies to a toe, since it is an assemblage of joints, and to a joint as well, because of its division into its own parts.

---

352. **Tibetan**: "...like perceiving a scarecrow as a person, due to its specific configuration."

353. **Tibetan**: "fingers" and "hand" instead of "toes" and "foot."

86. Even the parts can be divided into atoms, and an atom itself can be divided according to its cardinal directions. The section of a cardinal direction is space, because it is without parts. Therefore, an atom does not exist.[354]

87. What discerning person would be attached to form, which is just like a dream? Since the body does not exist, then who is a woman and who is a man?

88. If suffering truly exists, why does it not oppress the joyful? If delicacies and the like are a pleasure, why do they not please someone struck by grief and so forth?

89. If it is not experienced because it is overpowered by something more intense, how can that which is not of the nature of experience be a feeling?

90. *[Objection:]* Surely there is suffering in its subtle state while its gross state is removed.
[Mādhyamika:] If it is simply another pleasure, then that subtle state is a subtle state of pleasure.

91. If suffering does not arise when the conditions for its opposite have arisen, does it not follow that a "feeling" is a false notion created by conceptual fabrication?

92. Therefore, this analysis is created as an antidote to that false notion. For the meditative stabilizations that arise from the field of investigations are the food of contemplatives.

93. If there is an interval between a sense-faculty and its object, where is the contact between the two? If there is no interval, they would be identical. In that case, what would be in contact with what?

94. One atom cannot penetrate another, because it is without empty space and is of the same size as the other. When there is no penetration, there is no mingling; and when there is no mingling, there is no contact.

---

354. **Tibetan:** "...Since the cardinal directions have no parts, they are like space. Therefore, atoms do not exist."

95. How, indeed, can there be contact with something that has no parts? If partlessness can be observed when there is contact, demonstrate this.

96. It is impossible for consciousness, which has no form, to have contact; nor is it possible for a composite, because it is not a truly existent thing, as investigated earlier.

97. Thus, when there is no contact, how can feeling arise? What is the reason for this exertion? Who could be harmed by what?

98. If there is no one to experience feeling and if feeling does not exist, then after understanding this situation, why, O craving, are you not shattered?

99. The mind that has a dreamlike and illusionlike nature sees and touches. Since feeling arises together with the mind, it is not perceived by the mind.

100. What happens earlier is remembered but not experienced by what arises later. It does not experience itself, nor is it experienced by something else.

101. There is no one who experiences feeling. Hence, in reality, there is no feeling. Thus, in this identityless bundle, who can be hurt by it?

102. The mind is not located in the sense faculties, nor in form and other sense-objects, nor in between them. The mind is also not found inside, nor outside, nor anywhere else.

103. That which is not in the body nor anywhere else, neither intermingled nor somewhere separate, is nothing. Therefore, sentient beings are by nature liberated.[355]

---

355. According to the *Pañjikā*, pp. 245-246, the mind that is not in the body nor somewhere else outside the body, that is neither intermingled between those two, the body and outside thing, nor separate from the body and present somewhere else, is ultimately nothing, that is, it does not truly exist. It is only presented by mental fabrication. The *saṃsāric* mind appears like an illusion because it lacks an intrinsic nature. For that reason, sentient beings are liberated by nature, because the natural *nirvāṇa (prākṛti-nirvāṇa)*, which has the characteristic of the absence of intrinsic nature, is always present in the streams of consciousness of all sentient beings.

104. If cognition is prior to the object of cognition, in dependence on what does it arise? If cognition is simultaneous with the object of cognition, in dependence on what does it arise?

105. If it arises after the object of cognition, from what would cognition arise? In this way it is ascertained that no phenomenon comes into existence.

106. *[Objection:]* If conventional truth does not exist, how can there be the two truths? If it does exist due to another conventional truth, how can there be a liberated sentient being?

107. *[Mādhyamika:]* One is an ideation of someone else's mind, and one does not exist by one's own conventional truth. After something has been ascertained, it exists; if not, it does not exist as a conventional reality either.

108. The two, conception and the conceived, are mutually dependent, just as every analysis is expressed by referring to what is commonly known.

109. *[Objection:]* But if one analyzes by means of analysis which itself is analyzed, then there is an infinite regress, because that analysis can also be analyzed.

110. *[Mādhyamika:]* When the object of analysis is analyzed, no basis for analysis is left. Since there is no basis, it does not arise, and that is called *"nirvāṇa."*

111. A person for whom these two[356] are truly existent is in an extremely shaky position. If an object exists because of the power of cognition, how does one arrive at the true existence of cognition?

112. If cognition exists because of the power of the object of cognition, how does one arrive at the true existence of the object of cognition? If their existence is due to their mutual power, neither can exist.

113. *[Objection:]* If there is no father without a son, how can there be a son?

---

356. The *Pañjikā*, p. 250, "...i.e., analysis and the object of analysis."

[*Mādhyamika:*] Just as in the absence of a son there is no father, in the same way, those two[357] do not exist.

114. [*Objection:*] A sprout arises from a seed. The seed is indicated by that sprout. Why does cognition that arises from the object of cognition not ascertain the true existence of that object of cognition?

115. [*Mādhyamika:*] It is ascertained that a seed exists owing to a cognition that is not the same as a sprout. How is the existence of a cognition cognized, since the object of cognition is ascertained by that cognition?

116. People observe every cause through direct perception, since the components of a lotus, such as the stalk and so forth, are produced by a variety of causes.

117. [*Qualm:*] What makes the variety of causes?
[*Mādhyamika:*] A preceding variety of causes.
[*Qualm:*] How can a cause give an effect?
[*Mādhyamika:*] Because of the power of preceding causes.

118. [*Nyāya-Vaiśeṣika:*] Īśvara is the cause of the world.
[*Mādhyamika:*] Then explain who Īśvara is. If he is the elements, so be it; but then why the tussle over a mere name?

119. Moreover, the earth and other elements are not one; they are impermanent, inactive, and not divine. They can be stepped on and are impure. That is not Īśvara.

120. Space is not the Lord because it is inactive. Nor is it the Self, because that has been refuted. How can the inconceivable creatorship of the Inconceivable One be described?

121. What does he desire to create? If [he desires to create] a Self, are not that Self, the nature of the earth and other elements, and Īśvara eternal? Cognition is due to the object of cognition and is without beginning.

122. Happiness and suffering are the result of action. Say then, what did he create? If the cause has no beginning, how can its effect have a beginning?

---

357. The *Pañjikā*, p. 251, "...i.e., cognition and the object of cognition."

123. If he does not depend on anything else, why does he not always create? There is nothing whatsoever that is not created by him, so on what would he depend?

124. If Īśvara depends on a collection of conditions, then again, he is not the cause. He cannot refrain from creating when there is a collection of conditions, nor can he create in their absence.

125. If Īśvara creates without desiring to do so, it would follow that he is dependent on something other than himself. Even if he desires to create, he is dependent on that desire. Whence is the supremacy of the creator?

126. Those who claim that atoms are permanent[358] have been refuted earlier. The Sāṃkhyas consider a primal substance as the permanent cause of the world.

127. The universal constituents—*sattva*, *rajas*, and *tamas*—remaining in equilibrium, are called the primal substance. The universe is explained by their disequilibrium.

128. It is implausible that a single thing has three natures, so it does not exist. Likewise, the universal constituents do not exist, since they would each be comprised of three constituents.

129. In the absence of the three universal constituents, the existence of sound and other sense-objects is far-fetched. There is also no possibility of pleasure and the like in unconscious things such as cloth and so on.

130. If you argue that things have the nature of causes, have things not been analyzed away? For you, pleasure and the like are the cause, but cloth and the like are not a result of that cause.[359]

131. Happiness and other feelings may be due to things such as a cloth, but in their absence, there would be no happiness and so

---

358. According to the *Pañjikā*, p. 261, the Mīmāṃsakas and others.

359. *sPyod 'jug rnam bshad rgyal sras 'jug ngogs*, p. 267, explains that according to the Sāṃkhya view, the primal substance in which *sattva* (which Śāntideva refers to here as *pleasure*) and the other constituents are in equilibrium is the cause of things such as cloth, but Śāntideva refutes that cloth and so forth arise from that primal substance.

on. The permanence of happiness and other feelings is never ascertained.[360]

132. If the manifestation of happiness truly exists, why is the feeling not apprehended? If you say that it becomes subtle, how can it be gross and subtle?[361]

133. [Objection:] It is subtle upon leaving its gross state. Its grossness and subtlety are impermanent.
[Mādhyamika:] Why do you not consider everything as impermanent in that way?

134. If its gross state is not different from happiness, then the impermanence of happiness is obvious. If you think that something non-existent does not arise because it has no existence whatsoever, then you have accepted, even against your will, the origination of something manifest that was non-existent.

135. If you accept that the effect is present in the cause, then one who eats food would be eating excrement, and a cotton-tree seed would be bought at the price of a cloth and worn as a garment.

136. If you argue that ordinary people do not see this because of delusion, this is the case even for one who knows reality.

137. Even ordinary people know that. Why do they not see it? If you argue that ordinary people have no verifying cognition, then even their perception of something manifest is false.

138. [Sāṃkhya:] If verifying cognition is not verifying cognition, then is that not verified falsely? In reality, the emptiness of phenomena is not ascertained through that verifying cognition.[362]

---

360. sPyod 'jug rnam bshad rgyal sras 'jug ngogs, p. 267, comments that if joy and so forth were to arise from such things as cloth, in the absence of cloth and so forth, such feelings could not exist, for a result cannot occur without its cause.

361. sPyod 'jug rnam bshad rgyal sras 'jug ngogs, p. 267, comments that if the manifestation of happiness exists as a permanent entity, it would follow that the experience of happiness should be apprehended when suffering arises, for it is permanent. If the Sāṃkhyas assert that it fluctuates between subtle and coarse states, then it follows that feelings are not permanent as they maintain.

362. **Tibetan:** "If verifying cognition is not verifying cognition, then that which is known is false. In reality, the meditation on emptiness is therefore invalid."

139. *[Mādhyamika:]* Without detecting an imagined thing, its non-existence is not apprehended. Therefore, if a thing is false, its non-existence is clearly false.

140. Thus, when in a dream a son has died, the thought "He does not exist" prevents the arising of the thought of his existence; and that too is false.

141. Therefore, with this analysis, nothing exists without a cause, nor is it contained in its individual or combined causal conditions.

142. Nothing comes from something else, nothing remains, and nothing departs. What is the difference between an illusion and that which is considered by fools as real?

143. Examine this: As for that which is created by illusion and that which is created by causes, where do they come from and where do they go?

144. How can there be true existence in something artificial, like a reflection, which is perceived only in conjunction with something else and not in its absence?

145. For something that already exists, what need is there for a cause? If something does not exist, what is the need for a cause?

146. Something that does not exist will not be subject to change, even with millions of causes. How can something in that state be existent? What else can come into existence?

147. If there is no existent thing at the time of non-existence, when will an existent thing come into existence? For that non-existent thing will not disappear as long as the existent thing is not produced.

148. When a non-existent thing has not disappeared, there is no opportunity for the existent thing. An existent thing does not become non-existent, since it would follow that it would be of two natures.

149. Thus, there is neither cessation nor coming into existence at any time. Therefore, this entire world does not arise or cease.

150. States of existence are like dreams; upon analysis, they are similar to plantain trees. In reality, there is no difference between those who have attained *nirvāṇa* and those who have not.

151. When all phenomena are empty in this way, what can be gained and what can be lost? Who will be honored or despised by whom?

152. Whence comes happiness or suffering? What is pleasant and what is unpleasant? When investigated in its own nature, what is craving and for what is that craving?

153. Upon investigation, what is the world of living beings, and who will really die here? Who will come into existence, and who has come into existence? Who is a relative, and who is a friend of whom?

154. May those who are like me apprehend everything as being like space. They rage and rejoice by means of dispute and jubilation.[363]

155. Seeking their own happiness with evil deeds, they live miserably with grief, troubles, despair, and cutting and stabbing each other.[364]

156. After repeatedly entering the fortunate states of existence and becoming accustomed to pleasure again and again, they die and fall into the miserable states of existence in which there is long and intense anguish.

157. There are many pitfalls in mundane existence, but there is not this truth there. There is mutual incompatibility.[365] Reality could not be like this.

---

363. According to the *Pañjikā*, p. 276, "they" refers to "foolish people like me who do not know ultimate reality."

   Tibetan: "...Due to the causes of strife, those desiring their own happiness become angry, and due to the causes of revelry they rejoice."

364. **Tibetan:** "Agitated and delighted, they strive in misery, quarreling, slashing and stabbing one another, and lead their lives in troubles and vice."

365. According to the *sPyod 'jug rnam bshad rgyal sras 'jug ngogs*, p. 276, the incompatibility is between the understanding of reality and the state of being bound in mundane existence.

158. There are incomparable, violent, and boundless oceans of suffering. Strength is scanty there; and the life span is short there as well.

159. There, too, in practices for long life and health, in hunger, fatigue, and weariness, in sleep and calamities, and in unprofitable associations with fools,

160. Life passes by swiftly and in vain. Discrimination is difficult to obtain there. How could there be a way to prevent habitual distractions?

161. There, too, Māra[366] tries to throw them into very wretched states. There, because of the abundance of wrong paths, doubt is difficult to overcome,

162. And leisure is hard to obtain again. The appearance of a Buddha is extremely rare. The flood of mental afflictions is difficult to impede. Alas, what a succession of suffering!

163. Ah, there should be great pity for those adrift in the flood of suffering, who, although miserable in this way, do not recognize their wretched situation.

164. Just like one who repeatedly immerses himself in water but must enter fire again and again, so they consider themselves fortunate, although they are extremely miserable.

165. As they live like this, pretending that they are not subject to aging and death, terrible calamities come, with death the foremost of them.[367]

---

366. According to the *Pañjikā*, p. 278, Devaputra Māra, that is, the Māra of mental afflictions *(kleśa-māra)*.

367. **Tibetan:** "For those who live pretending that they are not subject to aging and death, first they are killed and then they fall into unbearable, miserable states of existence."

166. Thus, when might I bring relief to those tormented by the fire of suffering, with the requisites of happiness springing forth from the clouds of my merit?[368]

167. When shall I respectfully teach emptiness and the accumulation of merit—in terms of conventional truth and without reification—to those whose views are reified?[369]

---

368. **Tibetan:** "With the rain of the requisites of my well-being, which springs forth from the clouds of merit, when might I bring relief to those tormented by the fire of misery?"

369. **Tibetan:** "When might I reverently accumulate collections of merit without reification and reveal emptiness to those who are ruined by reification?"

Chapter X
Dedication

1. May all sentient beings be graced with the Bodhisattva way of life by the virtue I have obtained while reflecting on *A Guide to the Bodhisattva Way of Life.*[370]

2. Through my merit, may all those in all directions who are afflicted by bodily and mental sufferings obtain oceans of joy and contentment.

3. As long as the cycle of existence lasts, may their happiness never decline. May the world attain the constant joy of the Bodhisattvas.

4. As many hells as there are in the worlds, may beings in them delight in the joys of contentment in Sukhāvatī.

5. May those afflicted with cold find warmth. May those oppressed with heat be cooled by oceans of water springing from the great clouds of the Bodhisattvas.[371]

---

370. **Tibetan:** "Due to the virtue of my composing *A Guide to the Bodhisattva Way of Life*, may all beings enter the Bodhisattva way of life."

371. **Tibetan:** "May those afflicted with cold find warmth, and may those oppressed with heat be cooled by limitless streams of water from the great clouds of the Bodhisattvas."

6.   May the forest of sword-leaves become for them the splendor of a pleasure-grove; and may the swordlike Śālmalī trees grow as wish-fulfilling trees.[372]

7.   May the regions of hell become vast ponds of delight, fragrant with lotuses, beautiful and pleasing with the cries of white geese, wild ducks, ruddy geese, and swans.

8.   May the heap of burning coal become a mound of jewels. May the burning ground become a crystal marble floor; and may the mountains of "the crushing hell" become temples of worship filled with Sugatas.

9.   May the rain of burning coal, lava, and daggers from now on become a rain of flowers; and may mutual battling with weapons now become a playful flower-fight.

10.   By the power of my virtue, may those whose flesh has completely fallen off, whose skeletons are of the color of a white jasmine flower, and who are immersed in the river Vaitaraṇī whose water is like fire, attain celestial bodies and dwell with goddesses by the river Mandākinī.

11.   May the horrifying agents of Yama, crows, and vultures suddenly watch here in fear. Those looking upward behold blazing Vajrapāṇi in the sky and wonder: "Whose is this brilliant light that dispels darkness all around and generates the joy of contentment?" May they depart together with him, freed of vice through the power of their joy.[373]

12.   A rain of lotuses falls mixed with fragrant waters. It is seen to extinguish the unceasing fires of the hells. May the beings of

---

372. **Tibetan:** "May the forest of sword-leaves become for them a lovely pleasure-grove, and may the Śālmalī trees arise as wish-fulfilling trees."

373. **Tibetan:** "'Why are the horrifying agents of Yama, crows and vultures frightened here? By whose power is this glorious force that thoroughly dispels darkness and brings forth joy and delight?' With this thought, may beings look up and behold blazing Vajrapāṇi in the midst of the sky, and by the power of their ecstasy may they be freed of vice and depart with him."

the hells, suddenly refreshed with joy, wonder, What is this? and may they see Padmapāṇi.[374]

13. Friends, come, come quickly! Cast away fear! We are alive! A radiant vanquisher of fear, a certain prince in a monastic robe,[375] has come to us. By his power every adversity is removed, streams of delight flow, the Spirit of Awakening is born, as is compassion, the mother of protection of all beings.[376]

14. Behold him whose lotus-feet are worshiped with tiaras of hundreds of gods, whose eyes are moist with compassion, on whose head a stream of diverse flowers rains down, with his delightful summer palaces celebrated by thousands of goddesses singing hymns of praise. Upon seeing Mañjughoṣa before them, may the beings of the hells immediately cheer.

15. Through my virtues, may the beings of the hells rejoice upon seeing the unobscured clouds of Bodhisattvas, headed by Samantabhadra and bearing pleasant, cool, and fragrant rains and breezes.[377]

16. May the intense pains and fears of the beings of the hells be pacified. May the inhabitants of all miserable states of existence be liberated from their woeful states.[378]

---

374. **Tibetan:** "Upon seeing the burning, glowing embers of the hells extinguished by a rain of flowers mixed with scented water, and suddenly being refreshed with joy, may the beings of the hells wonder, What is this? and may they see Padmapāṇi."

375. *Cirikumāra*, translated here as "a prince in a monastic robe" is another name for Mañjughoṣa, or Mañjuśrī.

376. **Tibetan:** "Friends, cast aside your fear and come quickly! To us has come the radiant Cirikumāra, by whose power all suffering is removed, the force of gladness is exuded, all beings are protected, the Spirit of Awakening and compassion arise, and fear is vanquished."

377. **Tibetan:** "On account of the roots of my virtue, may the beings of the hells rejoice upon seeing the pleasant, cool, fragrant rain fall from the unobscured clouds of Bodhisattvas such as Samantabhadra."

378. This verse is missing in the Tibetan translation.

17. May the animals' risk of being eaten by each other disappear. May the *pretas* be as happy as the people in Uttarakuru.[379]

18. May the *pretas* always be satiated, bathed, and refreshed by the streams of milk pouring from the hand of noble Avalokiteśvara.

19. May the blind always see forms, and may the deaf hear. May pregnant women give birth without pains, as did Māyādevī.

20. May they acquire everything that is beneficial and desired by the mind: clothing, food, drink, flower garlands, sandal-paste, and ornaments.[380]

21. May the fearful become fearless and those struck by grief find joy. May the despondent become resolute and free of trepidation.[381]

22. May the ill have good health. May they be freed from every bondage. May the weak become strong and have affectionate hearts for one another.[382]

23. May all regions be advantageous to all those who travel on roads. May the purpose for which they set out be expediently accomplished.[383]

24. May those who journey by boat succeed as they desire. May they safely reach the shore and rejoice with their relatives.[384]

---

379. Uttarakuru is, according to one tradition, the most northerly of the four main divisions of the known world, and according to another tradition, it is one of the nine divisions of the world, often described as a country of everlasting happiness.

380. **Tibetan:** "May the naked acquire clothing, the hungry acquire food, and the thirsty acquire water and delicious drinks."

381. **Tibetan:** "May the destitute attain wealth, and may those struck by grief find delight. May those who despair be inspired and imbued with enormous fortitude."

382. **Tibetan:** "May all sentient beings who are ill swiftly be free of disease. May every illness of the world never arise again."

383. **Tibetan:** "May those who are frightened be fearless, and may those who are in shackles be released. May the weak be imbued with strength, and may their hearts be dear to one another." The next verse in the Tibetan reads: "May all directions be felicitous for all travelers. May the purpose for which they set out be accomplished effortlessly."

384. **Tibetan:** "May those who have set out in boats and ships accomplish their aims, and upon safely returning to shore, may they rejoice together with their relatives."

25. May those who find themselves on wrong paths in dreary forests come upon the company of fellow travelers; and without fatigue, may they journey without fear of bandits, tigers, and the like.[385]

26. May deities protect the dull, the insane, the deranged, the helpless, the young, and the elderly, and those in danger from sickness, the wilderness, and so on.[386]

27. May they be free from all lack of leisure; may they be endowed with faith, wisdom, and compassion; may they be possessed of stature and good conduct; and may they always remember their former lives.[387]

28. May they be inexhaustible treasuries just like Sky-treasure. Free of conflict or irritation, may they have an independent way of life.[388]

29. May beings who have little splendor be endowed with great magnificence. May unattractive wretches be endowed with beauty.

30. May the women in the world become men. May the lowly obtain grandeur and yet be free of arrogance.

31. Through this merit of mine, may all beings without exception abstain from every vice and always engage in virtue.

---

385. **Tibetan:** "May those who have wandered onto miserable, wrong paths meet with fellow travelers, and may they journey at ease, without fear of bandits, tigers, and so on, and without fatigue."

386. **Tibetan:** "May deities protect children, the aged, the unprotected, the stupefied, the deranged, and the insane who are tragically in a trackless wilderness and so on."

387. **Tibetan:** "May beings be free from all absences of leisure; may they be endowed with faith, wisdom, and kindness; and with fine food and conduct may they always remember their former lives."

388. Sky-treasure, or Gaganagañja, is the name of a Bodhisattva.
    Tibetan: "May the enjoyments of everyone be unceasing like the treasury of the sky. Without conflict and without harm, may they live freely."

32. Not lacking the Spirit of Awakening, devoted to the Bodhisattva way of life, embraced by the Buddhas, and free of the deeds of Māras,

33. May all beings have immeasurable life spans. May they always live happily, and may even the word "death" disappear.

34. May all quarters of the world be delightful with gardens of wish-fulfilling trees, filled with the Buddhas and the Children of the Buddhas, and be enchanting with the sounds of Dharma.[389]

35. May the ground everywhere be free from stones and rocks, smooth like the palm of the hand, soft and made of lapis lazuli.

36. May the great assemblies of Bodhisattvas sit on all sides. May they beautify the earth with their own resplendence.

37. May all beings unceasingly hear the sound of Dharma from the birds, from every tree, from the rays of light, and from the sky.

38. May they always encounter the Buddhas and the Children of the Buddhas. May they worship the Spiritual Mentor of the World with endless clouds of offerings.

39. May a god send rain in time, and may there be an abundance of crops. May the populace be prosperous, and may the king be righteous.

40. May medicines be effective, and may the mantras of those who recite them be successful. May *ḍākiṇīs*, *rākṣasas*, and other ghouls be filled with compassion.

41. May no sentient being be unhappy, sinful, ill, neglected,[390] or despised; and may no one be despondent.

42. May monasteries be well established, full of chanting and study. May there always be harmony among the Saṅgha, and may the purpose of the Saṅgha be accomplished.

---

389. **Tibetan:** "May all quarters of the world be occupied with groves of wish-fulfilling trees filled with Buddhas and the Children of the Buddhas sweetly proclaiming the Dharma."

390. The **Tibetan** reads "frightened" instead of "neglected."

43. May monks who wish to practice find solitude. May they meditate with their minds agile and free of all distractions.

44. May nuns receive provisions and be free of quarrels and troubles. May all renunciates be of untarnished ethical discipline.

45. May those who are of poor ethical discipline be disgusted and become constantly intent on the extinction of their vices. May they reach a fortunate state of existence, and may their vows remain unbroken there.

46. May they be learned and cultured, receive alms, and have provisions. May their mind-streams be pure and their fame be proclaimed in every direction.[391]

47. Without experiencing the suffering of the miserable states of existence and without arduous practice, may the world attain Buddhahood in a single divine body.[392]

48. May all sentient beings worship all the Buddhas in many ways. May they be exceedingly joyful with the inconceivable bliss of the Buddhas.

49. May the Bodhisattvas' wishes for the welfare of the world be fulfilled; and whatever the Protectors intend for sentient beings, may that be accomplished.

50. May the Pratyekabuddhas and Śrāvakas be happy, always worshiped by the lofty gods, *asuras*, and humans.[393]

51. Through the grace of Mañjughoṣa, may I always achieve ordination and the recollection of past lives until I reach the Joyous Ground.[394]

---

391. **Tibetan:** "May the learned be honored and provided with alms. May their mind-streams be pure, and may they be renowned in all the quarters of the world."

392. **Tibetan:** "Without experiencing the suffering of the miserable states of existence, and without arduous practice, may they swiftly attain Buddhahood with a body superior to that of the gods."

393. The Tibetan version lacks the second clause.

394. *Pramuditā-bhūmi*, the first Bodhisattva Ground.

52.   May I live endowed with strength in whatever posture I am. In all my lives may I find plentiful places of solitude.[395]

53.   When I wish to see or ask something, may I see the Protector Mañjunātha himself, without any impediment.

54.   May my way of life be like that of Mañjuśrī, who lives to accomplish the benefit of all sentient beings throughout the ten directions.

55.   For as long as space endures and for as long as the world lasts, may I live dispelling the miseries of the world.

56.   Whatever suffering there is for the world, may it all ripen upon me. May the world find happiness through all the virtues of the Bodhisattvas.[396]

57.   May the teaching that is the sole medicine for the suffering of the world and the source of all prosperity and joy remain for a long time, accompanied by riches and honor.

58.   I bow to Mañjughoṣa, through whose grace my mind turns to virtue. I salute my spiritual friend through whose kindness it becomes stronger.[397]

---

395. **Tibetan:** "May I survive and be strong even with coarse food. In all my lives may I find excellent places of solitude."

396. **Tibetan:** "...and may the world experience happiness through the community of Bodhisattvas."

397. **Tibetan:** "...I also bow to my spiritual friend, through whose kindness I develop."

Bibliography of Śāntideva's Works and Commentaries on His Works

I. SANSKRIT EDITIONS OF ŚĀNTIDEVA'S WORKS

Bodhicaryāvatāra

1889. *Bodhicaryāvatāra.* Edited by I. Minayef. In *Zapiski Vostochnogo Otdeleniya Ruskogo Imperatorskogo Archeologicheskogo Obchestva (Transactions of the Oriental Section of the Royal Russian Archeological Society)*, vol. 4.

1898. *Ādikarmapradīpa, Bodhicaryāvatāraṭīkā.* Edited by Louis de la Vallée Poussin. In *Bouddhisme, Études et Materiaux*, vol. 1. Bruxelles, London: Academie and Luzac. (Includes only the ninth chapter of the text.)

1901–1914. *Bodhicaryāvatārapañjikā. Commentary to the Bodhicaryāvatāra of Śāntideva.* Edited by Louis de la Vallée Poussin. Biblioteca Indica, no. 150. Calcutta: The Asiatic Society. (Includes only the first nine chapters of the text.)

1901. *Prajñākaramati's Commentary to the Bodhicāryāvatāra of Śāntideva.* Edited with Indices by Louis de la Vallée Poussin. Bibliotheca Indica. New Series, no. 983. Calcutta: Asiatic Society of Bengal.

1960. *Bodhicaryāvatāra of Śāntideva with the Commentary Pañjikā of Prajñākaramati.* Edited by P. L. Vaidya. Buddhist Sanskrit Texts, no. 12. Darbhanga: The Mithila Institute of Post-Graduate Studies and Research in Sanskrit Learning.

1960. *Bodhicaryāvatāra*. Edited by Vidhushekhara Bhattacharya. Biblioteca Indica, no. 280. Calcutta: The Asiatic Society. (Sanskrit text together with the Tibetan version.)

1988. *Bodhicaryāvatāra with Prajñakaramati's Commentary*. Edited by Dwaraka Das Shastri. Bauddha Bharati Series, no. 21. Varanasi: Chandra Prakash Press.

Śikṣāsamuccaya

1902. *Śikṣāsamuccaya: A Compendium of Buddhist Teaching Compiled by Śāntideva Chiefly from Earlier Mahāyāna-Sūtras*. Edited by Cecil Bendall. St. Petersburg: Imperial Academy of Sciences. Vol. 39-47. Reprinted in 1970.

1956. *Śāntideva's Śikṣāsamuccaya-kārikās*. Edited and translated into English by Lal Mani Joshi. Sarnath: Mahabodhi Society.

1961. *Śikṣāsamuccaya*. Edited by P. L. Vaidya. Buddhist Sanskrit Texts, no. 11. Darbhanga: The Mithila Institute of Post-Graduate Studies and Research in Sanskrit Learning.

II. TRANSLATIONS OF ŚĀNTIDEVA'S WORKS

Bodhicaryāvatāra: Asian Languages

Bodhicaryāvatāra, Byang chub sems dpa'i spyod pa la 'jug pa. Derge: La 1.2.

Bodhicaryāvatāra: Mongolskii perevod Chos-kyi hod-zer'a. 1929. Edited by B. Vladimirtsov. Bibliotheca Buddhica, vol. 28. Leningrad: Izdalestvo Akademii Nauk SSSR.

Byang chub sems dpa'i spyod pa la 'jug pa. No. 3871 in *A Complete Catalogue of the Tibetan Buddhist Canons*. 1934. Edited by H. Ui, M. Suzuki, Y. Kanakura, and T. Tada. Sendai, Japan: Tōhoku Imperial University by Saitō Gratitude Foundation. Second edition printed in 1970, Tokyo.

Byang chub sems dpa'i spyod pa la 'jug pa. Peking edition of the *Tibetan Tripiṭaka*, no. 5272, vol. 99.

Kanakura, Y. 1958. *Satori eno Michi*. Kyoto: Heirakuji Shoten. (Japanese)
Poppe, Nicholas. 1954. "A Fragment of the *Bodhicaryāvatāra* from Olon Sume." *Harvard Journal of Asiatic Studies* 17: 411-418. (Mongolian)

Pu ti xing jing. No. 1662 in the *Taishō shinshū daizōkyō.* 1924-32. Edited by J. Takakusu, K. Watanabe, et al. Tokyo: Taishō Issaikyō Kankō Kai.

Bodhicaryāvatāra: Western Languages

Barnett, Lionel David. 1909. *The Path of Light.* New York: Grove; London: John Murray. Second edition published in 1947, London: John Murray.

Batchelor, Stephen. 1979. *A Guide to the Bodhisattva's Way of Life.* Dharamsala: Library of Tibetan Works and Archives. Second edition published in 1981.

Crosby, Kate, and Andrew Skilton. 1996. *Śāntideva. The Bodhicaryāvatāra.* The World's Classics. Oxford, New York: Oxford University Press.

Ensink, J. 1955. *De grote weg naar het licht: Een keuze uit de literatuur van het Mahāyāna Buddhisme.* Uit het Sanskrit vertaald en toegelicht. Amsterdam: De Arbeiderspers. Second edition published in 1973, Amsterdam: Wetenschappelijke Uitgereij. (Chapter 2)

Finot, Louis. 1920. *La Marche à la lumière: Bodhicaryāvatāra.* Les classiques de l'Orient, vol. 2. Paris: Editions Bossard.

La Vallée Poussin, Louis de. 1892. "*Bodhicaryāvatāra:* Introduction à la pratique de la sainteté bouddhique." *Muséon* 11: 87-115. Reprinted in 1896. (Chapters 1-4, 10)

—. 1896. "Śāntideva: *Bodhicaryāvatāra.* Expos. de la pratique des Bodhisattvas (Tr. du cinquième Pariccheda)." *Muséon* 15: 306-18. (Chapter 5)

—. 1907. *Bodhicaryāvatāra: Introduction à la pratique des future Buddhas: Poème de Śāntideva.* Paris: Librairie Blond.

Lindtner, Christian. 1981. *To buddhistiske laeredigte.* Indiske Studier, vol. 1, pp. 36-162. Copenhagen: I Kommision hos Akademisk Forlag.

Matics, Marion L. 1970. *Entering the Path of Enlightenment.* London: Macmillan.

Pezzali, Amalia. 1975. *Il Bodhicaryāvatāra di Śāntideva.* Bologna: Egidi.

Śāstri, N. Aiyaswami. 1950. "Epitome of the *Bodhicaryāvatāra* with Its Pañjikā." *Adyar Library Bulletin* 17: 36-441. (Chapter 10)

Schmidt, Richard. 1923. *Der Eintritt in den Wandel in Erlechtung (Bodhi-caryāvatāra)*. Von Śāntideva. Ein buddhistisches Lehrgedicht des VII. Jahrhunderts n. Chr. Aus dem Sanskrit übersetzt. Dokumente der Religion, vol. 5. Paderborn: Ferdinand Schöning.

Sharma, Parmananda. 1990. *Bodhicaryāvatāra*, 2 vols. New Delhi: Aditya Prakashan.

Steinkellner, Ernst. 1981. *Śāntideva: Eintritt in das Leben zur Erlechtung (Bodhicaryāvatāra)*. Lehrgedicht des Mahāyāna aus dem Sanskrit übersetzt von Ernst Steinkellner. Diederichs Gelbe Reihe, vol. 34. Düsseldorf: Eugen Diederichs.

Tucci, Giuseppe. 1925. *In camino verso la luce*. Torino. (Chapters 1-8)

Wallace, B. Alan, tr. and ed. 1988. *Transcendent Wisdom*. The Ninth Chapter of the Shantideva's *Guide to the Bodhisattva Way of Life* with a Commentary by H. H. the Dalai Lama, Tenzin Gyatso. Ithaca, New York: Snow Lion.

Śikṣāsamuccaya: Asian Languages

Da cheng ji pu sa xue lun. No. 1636 in the *Taishō shinshū daizōkyō*. 1924-32. Edited by J. Takakusu, K. Watanabe, et al. Tokyo: Taishō Issaikyō Kankō Kai.

bSlab pa kun las btus pa. No. 3940 in *A Complete Catalogue of the Tibetan Buddhist Canons*. 1934. Edited by H. Ui, M. Suzuki, Y. Kanakura, and T. Tada. Sendai, Japan: Tōhoku Imperial University by Saitō Gratitude Foundation. Second edition printed in 1970, Tokyo.

bSlab pa kun las btus pa'i tshig le'ur byas pa. No. 3939 in *A Complete Catalogue of the Tibetan Buddhist Canons*. 1934. Edited by H. Ui, M. Suzuki, Y. Kanakura, and T. Tada. Sendai, Japan: Tōhoku Imperial University by Saitō Gratitude Foundation. Second edition printed in 1970, Tokyo. (Contains only *kārikās*)

bSlab pa kun las btus pa'i tshig le'ur byas pa. Peking edition of the Tibetan Tripiṭaka, vol. 102, no. 5336.

Śikṣāsamuccaya: Western Languages

Barnett, Lionel David. 1909. *The Path of Light*. New York: Grove; London: John Murray. Second edition published in 1947, London: John Murray, pp. 103-107, Appendix.

Bendall, Cecil, and W. H. D. Rouse. 1981. *Śikṣā-samuccaya: A Compendium of Buddhist Doctrine Compiled by Śāntideva, Chiefly from Earlier Mahāyāna Sūtras*. Delhi, Vanarasi, Patna: Motilal Banarsidass. First edition published in London: John Murray, 1922.

Joshi, Lal Mani. 1977. *Studies in the Buddhistic Culture of India: During the 7th and 8th centuries AD*. Delhi, Varanasi, Patna: Motilal Banarsidass. (Contains only *kārikās*, pp. 97-99)

Pezzali, Amalia. 1982. *Śāntideva, il Bodhicaryāvatāra e le Kārikā del Śikṣāsamuccaya*. Biblioteca Scientifica, vol. 11. Bologna: Editrice Missionaria Italiana.

Sūtrasamuccaya: Asian Languages

Fahu. *Ta ch'eng Pao Yao Yilun*. No. 1643 in *Taishō shinshū daizōkyō*. 1924-32. Edited by J. Takakusu, K. Watanabe et al. Tokyo: Taishō Issaikyō Kankō Kai.

III. COMMENTARIES AND SUMMARIES OF ŚĀNTIDEVA'S WORKS

Bodhicaryāvatāra

rGyal tshab dar ma rin chen. 1973. *sPyod 'jug rnam bshad rgyal sras 'jug ngogs*. Vāraṇasi: mThog slob dge ldan spyi las khang.

Gyatso, Kelsang. 1989. *Meaningful to Behold*. London: Tharpa.

Gyatso, Tenzin, the Fourteenth Dalai Lama. 1994. *A Flash of Lightning in the Dark of Night: A Guide to the Bodhisattva's Way of Life*. Translated from the Tibetan by the Padmakara Translation Group. Boston, London: Shambhala.

Ishida, Chikō. 1988. "Some New Remarks on the *Bodhicaryāvatāra* Chap. V." *Journal of Indian and Buddhist Studies* 37, no. 1.

Kajihara, Meiko. 1992. "On the *Pariṇāmanā* Chapter of the *Bodhicaryāvatāra*." *Journal of Indian and Buddhist Studies* 40, no. 20.

mKhan po kun bzang dpal ldan. 1982. *Byang chub sems dpa'i spyod pa la 'jug pa'i tshig 'grel 'jam dbyangs bla ma'i zhal lung bdud rtsi'i thig pa*. Paro, Bhutan: Kyichu Temple.

Saito, Akira. 1993. "A Study of Akṣayamati (=Śāntideva)'s *Bodhi-sattvacaryāvatāra* as Found in the Tibetan Manuscripts from Tun-huang." A Report of the Grant-in-Aid for Scientific Research (C). Mie, Japan.

Saito, Akira. 1994. "On the Difference between the Earlier and the Current Versions of Śāntideva's *Bodhi(sattva)caryāvatāra*, with Special Reference to Chap. 9 (/8) Entitled: 'Perfection of Wisdom (*prajñāpāramitā*).'" Research paper presented at IXth World Sanskrit Conference held on 9th to 15th January 1994 in Melbourne, Australia.

Sweet, Michael. 1976. "Śāntideva and the Mādhyamika: The Prajñāpāramitā-pariccheda of the *Bodhicaryāvatāra*." Ph.D. dissertation, University of Wisconsin.

Thogs med bzang po. 1974. *Byang chub sems dpa'i spyod pa la 'jug pa'i 'grel pa legs par bshad pa'i rgya mtsho*. Sarnath.

Thub bstan chos kyi grags pa. 1988. *Byang chub sems pa'i spyod pa la 'jug pa'i 'grel bshad rgyal sras rgya mtsho'i yon tan rin po che mi zad 'jo ba'i bum bzang*. Krung go'i bod kyi shes rin dpe skrun khang.

Wisdom: Two Buddhist Commentaries on the Ninth Chapter of Shantideva's Bodhicharyavatara (Khenchen Kunzang Palden: *The Nectar of Mañjushri's Speech*; Minyak Kunzang Sönam: *The Brilliant Torch*). 1993. Translated from the Tibetan by the Padmakara Translation Group. Peyzac-le-Moustier: Padmakara.

IV. INDICES TO THE *BODHICARYĀVATĀRA*

Takashi, Hirano. 1966. *An Index to the Bodhicaryāvatāra-pañjikā, chapter IX*. Tokyo: The Suzuki Foundation.

Weller, F. 1952. *Tibetisch-Sanskritischer Index zum Bodhicaryāvatāra. Abhandlungen der Sächsischen Akademie der Wissenschaften zu Leipzig.* Phil.-hist. Klasse, Band 46, Heft 3. Berlin: Akademie Verlag.

V. WRITINGS ON ŚĀNTIDEVA

Bu ston. 1986. "The Biography of the Bodhisattva Śāntideva." In the *History of Buddhism in India and Tibet*, pp. 161-166. Translated by E. Obermiller. Bibliotheca Indo-Buddhica, no. 26. Delhi: Sri Satguru Publications. First edition Heidelberg, 1932.

Chimpa, Lama, and Alaka Chattopadhyaya, trs. 1990. *Tāranātha's History of Buddhism in India*, pp. 215-220. Delhi: Motilal Banarsidass. First edition Simla, 1970.

de Jong, J. W. 1975. "La Légende de Śāntideva." *Indo-Iranian Journal* 16, no. 3: 161-182.

Pezzali, Amalia. 1968. *Śāntideva: mystique bouddhiste des VIIe et VIIIe siècle*. Firenze: Vallecchi Editore.